gel
candles

40 creative projects

C. Kaila Westerman

Photography by Giles D. Prett

STOREY
BOOKS

North Adams,
Massachusetts

The mission of Storey Publishing is to serve our customers by publishing practical
information that encourages personal independence in harmony with the environment.

Edited by Deborah Balmuth and Karen Levy
Cover design by Mark Tomasi
Candle styling by Karen Levy
Book design and production by Mark Tomasi
Photo styling by Karen Levy, Giles D. Prett, and Mark Tomasi
Indexed by Deborah Burns
Thanks to Starrville Soap Works of Tyler, Texas, for the donation of gel candlemaking supplies.

Printed in Hong Kong by C&C Offset
10 9 8 7 6 5 4 3 2 1

Library of Congress Cataloging-in-Publication Data

Westerman, C. Kaila (Carolyn Kaila), 1959-
    Gel Candles / by C. Kaila Westerman.
        p. cm.
    Includes index.
    ISBN 1-58017-390-X (alk. paper)
    1. Candlemaking. I. Title

    TT896.5 . W467 2001
    745.593'32--dc21

                                                    2001020963

contents

dedication

This book is dedicated to my husband, Trung Bui, who was gracious enough to emigrate from Vietnam just in time to marry me and provide structure and focus to my creative urges. This book is also dedicated to my parents, Dick and Phyllis Westerman. Thanks for being such fun folks.

acknowledgments

Many thanks to my editors, Deborah Balmuth and Karen Levy, and all the folks at Storey Books. Your faith and interest have allowed me to write this book.

preface

Candle crafting has been a popular hobby for decades, and it's no surprise why. Candles add a warm, aromatic, celebratory note to our lives. Over the years, the creativity and imagination of candlemakers have resulted in a wide variety of interesting candles on the market, as well as plenty of books and articles on the craft of candlemaking.

But most of what you see or read about are either solid candles made from beeswax, paraffin, or other waxes or liquid candles made from combustible oil. Candle gel, the craft world's newest innovation, is neither completely solid nor completely liquid. It is combustible mineral oil gelled with plastic resin, resulting in an ultra-transparent and long-burning alternative to wax.

Candle gel is definitely the brash new kid in town. It takes to bright colors with the retro-enthusiasm of Jell-O, and its transparency provides the perfect medium with which to create fanciful montages. Candle gel loves to dress up in glitter and to devilishly twist light with the complexity of a gemstone. This fresh, new medium is completely open to your creativity, and the candles you craft will elicit the *oohs* and *aahs* of friends who have "never seen anything like it!"

In addition to being an exciting new craft medium, candle gel is a blessedly easy material with which to work. If you have ever made candles with beeswax, paraffin, or other waxes, you know that it can be a messy endeavor. The tools used in candlemaking are forever coated in wax, and spills on the countertop or clothing are a real headache to remove.

Not so with candle gel. You can peel this material right off almost any surface, just as easily and completely as if you were peeling a piece of gelatin off a spoon. In fact, if you make a candle and don't like the way it looks, you can simply peel it out of the container and remelt it for another try. As an added bonus, candle gel has a much longer burning time than standard waxes, making for cost-effective candles.

Crafting with candle gel is extremely easy to master. After you read the basic information and make a couple of simple candles, you'll have all the confidence you need to tackle the more advanced projects. And, quickly thereafter, you will find it easy to use the photographs in this book as mere touchstones for your own innovations.

Whether you are a beginning or an experienced candle crafter, you are guaranteed to be knee deep in candlemaking within a few short hours of starting this book — and having a blast.

Enjoy!

10 easy
steps

Gel candle crafting is far simpler and less messy than candlemaking with traditional waxes. Gel is easy to handle — you just cut it with scissors or tear it with your hands. Unlike paraffin wax, which turns a lighter shade as it dries, candle gel is easy to color with candle dyes — what you see is what you get.

No matter which candle project you make, the basic steps are always the same; you simply vary the colors, scents, containers, and embedments. Once you've learned the 10 easy steps of gel candle crafting, you'll be ready to tackle the simple projects in the next chapter and then the more complicated projects that follow.

what is
candle gel?

Candle gel is not a wax. Like paraffin, it is made from hydrocarbons, but rather than being solid and white, candle gel has a soft, gelatin-like consistency and is crystal clear.

Candle gel has two big advantages over traditional paraffin waxes. First, the gel burns three to four times longer than paraffin, making it more cost-effective. Second, the gel is transparent, which allows the crafter to create some really fabulous designs that look completely different than those of traditional wax candles.

Most candle gel products have one important limitation, however. Since they are not solid like paraffin wax, they can't stand alone as a taper or pillar candle. Instead, they are usually cast into some type of container. This isn't really a drawback, though, as selecting and decorating the containers is a fun part of gel candle design.

Candle gel, made of mineral oil and resin, is transparent and has a gelatin-like consistency.

types of gel

There are different types of candle gel. Penreco Company, a large firm that has been working with petrochemicals for more than a hundred years, manufactures a product called Versagel C. This candle gel product comes in three densities: low polymer (LP), medium polymer (MP), and high polymer (HP).

LP candle gel is the least viscous of the three gels, which means your candles are less likely to contain excessive bubbles (bubbles will quickly become one of your main concerns in gel candle crafting). On the other hand, LP candle gel can only hold 0–4 percent fragrance (see page 27 for more information on fragrances) and it can be so thin that decorative embedments have a hard time staying suspended. Also, LP candle gel tends to pull away from the sides of the container, causing it to slip out if the container is turned upside down. This can be a problem if you ship the candles to a friend or customer, or if you sell them to a store where people may manhandle your creations.

In the middle of the hierarchy is MP candle gel, which holds 3–5 percent fragrance and suspends embedments and decorative glitter very well. This gel also strikes a nice middle ground with regard to bubbles and durability.

Finally there is HP candle gel, which holds high fragrance loads of up to 6 percent. It is much easier to suspend embedments in HP candle gel, and the candle is tougher when it comes to the abuses of shipping and the curious prodding of customers. On the down side, HP candle gel forms lots of bubbles as it cools. Most crafters prefer to work with MP or HP candle gel.

In addition to purchasing premade candle gel, you can purchase the raw materials of oil and resin to make it from scratch. Making candle gel from scratch is not a very difficult process (see the Appendix for general instructions and a list of suppliers that carry the raw materials). However, it does add an extra step to the creative process and introduces another opportunity for error.

The advantage to making your own gel is that you can greatly adjust the density of the finished product. For example, you can increase the density to the point at which the candle gel can stand alone without a container. Alternatively, you can reduce the density so that the gel has a viscosity like that of honey. You can then squeeze the low-density gel into a container without heating it up; this is a safer crafting material for children.

equipment

Most of the equipment you'll need for gel candle crafting can be found in the recesses of your kitchen cabinets or basement workshop. Here's the minimum that is required.

the essentials

▶ A means of melting the gel. Unlike traditional waxes that require double boilers, candle gel is melted over direct heat. Crafters usually melt the gel on their stovetops, in a medium-sized metal or glass pot. This direct-heat method is safe even if you use a gas stove, as long as you pay constant attention to the melting gel. Regardless of the type of stove you use, the gel should never be allowed to overheat or spill onto the burner. A safer option is to heat the gel in a freestanding electric pot with a temperature gauge, such as a deep fryer or a Presto cooker.

▶ A candle or candy thermometer that measures above 300°F. Candle gel is flammable and keeping an eye on the temperature as it melts will make your kitchen or workshop a safer place. Please do not work without an adequate thermometer.

▶ Basic utensils, including a stirring spoon for the gel and a teaspoon for measuring fragrances. Try to use metal utensils, as plastic runs the risk of melting in the hot gel and wood can retain water, resulting in a cloudy candle.

▶ Potholders. Since you will be working at temperatures of 200–250°F, potholders are a necessity.

▶ Colorants. Use wax-soluble colorants specifically made for candles. These come in chip, powder, and liquid forms. Liquid is the preferred form, since it is easiest to add to the gel. Some stores also carry liquid dyes specifically for gel candle crafting. Wax-based crayons will work in a pinch, but they contain opaque paraffin wax, so your candles will lose their transparency. Water-soluble colorants, such as food dye, and powdered pigments, micas, and pearlescents are not appropriate for gel candles. For recommendations on how to use color to best advantage, see page 29.

▶ Fragrances. Use only fragrances that are approved for gel candles. Don't use your favorite perfume. For more information on fragrances, see page 27.

▶ A candle container. Candle gel typically requires a container, since normally it is unable to stand on its own. For a detailed discussion of containers and appropriate container materials, see page 18.

▶ A wick. Your choice of wick is very important. The wick must be the right size or the candle will not burn well. Also, the wick must be self-tabbed with a metal holder that stands 7/16 inch (10mm) high. Please refer to page 21 for detailed information.

▸ Newspaper and paper towels. Spread the newspaper over your work surface to protect it from spilled perfumes and dyes. While the candle gel will probably peel right off any smooth countertop, the newspaper makes cleaning up easier. Paper towels come in handy during cleanup and for wiping down utensils.

▸ Scissors to trim the wick and cut the gel into chunks.

▸ Fire safety tools. These can include a fire extinguisher, a pot top, or a box of baking soda. Before beginning your gel candle adventure, it is essential that you read and understand the fire safety information on page 13.

The basic equipment: stovetop or hot plate; melting pot; fire safety equipment, such as baking soda; fragrance oil; container; paper towels; measuring cup; potholders; scissors; measuring spoons; candle dye; candle thermometer; wick; and stirring spoons.

the accessories

Glass pitchers, bamboo skewers, fine fishing line, and a heat gun will come in very handy.

As you advance in the craft, you'll find the following tools immeasurably helpful:

▶ Glass pitchers and a hot plate. Since you'll probably want to make candles with more than one color, it's convenient to melt batches of different colors at the same time. The easiest way to do this is to put several glass pitchers on a hot plate, with each one containing a color.

▶ A scale or measuring cups. These devices are helpful in keeping detailed records of your recipes and for measuring the proper amount of gel for a project.

▶ Poking utensils and thread. Tools for poking, prodding, and placing embedments are helpful. Bamboo skewers work well, but metal skewers or dental tools

are even better. Chopsticks are an excellent tool for positioning wicks and embedments in candle containers. Thread, fishing line, or fine metal wire can be used to temporarily suspend embedments until the gel cools. Then you simply pull the thread out.

▶ A metal cookie sheet or glass cutting board. For some projects, a flat metal or glass surface will be necessary.

▶ Craft paper, wax paper, and foil. For some projects, these will be helpful.

▶ A clean oven or a hair dryer, heat gun, or heat lamp. These devices are used to reduce bubbles and remove imperfections in the candle. For detailed information on heat techniques, see page 38.

gel candle crafting

Gel candle crafting can be done in 10 easy steps. You may find that you wish to change the order in which you do things or even skip some of the steps, depending on your project or personal preferences. However, if you are new to gel candle crafting, follow the order of these 10 steps until you feel comfortable with the process.

10 easy steps

Step 1: Set up the workspace.

Step 2: Prepare the container.

Step 3: Set the wick.

Step 4: Melt the gel.

Step 5: Add fragrance.

Step 6: Add color.

Step 7: Position embedments.

Step 8: Pour the gel and let it cool.

Step 9: Finish the candle and attach a warning label.

Step 10: Clean up.

1: set up the workspace

Assemble your materials and cover your work surface with newspaper.

2: prepare the container

Wash your container with soap and water and dry it thoroughly with a lint-free cloth. If you wish, wipe the inside and the outside with some rubbing alcohol, vinegar, or commercial glass cleaner to remove fingerprints and the last bit of soapy residue.

Use rubbing alcohol or another glass cleaner to wipe the glass free of fingerprints.

3: set the wick

Your choice of wick is very important to your success at crafting a safe and evenly burning candle. Detailed information on wick types is found on page 21. Once you have chosen the proper wick, trim it so that it stands about 1 inch higher than the mouth of the container. If it is too short or too long, you'll find it hard to keep it in place while the gel cools. Next, straighten the wick out with your fingers. If the wick isn't straight, your candle will burn off center as it follows the wick's curve. Also, since you are working with a transparent medium, people will see that the wick is not straight and the candle may look odd.

Finally, set the wick in the container by using one of the following methods:

▶ Use fast-setting clear epoxy glue to adhere the wick to the bottom of the container. Make sure the glue is completely dry and hard before you pour in the melted gel, or the glue will contaminate the gel and make it appear cloudy.

▶ Use Sticky Wicky or a bit of clay to adhere the wick to the bottom of the container. Use these products sparingly, though, as they can contaminate the clarity of the gel.

▶ Pour a little melted candle gel into the bottom of the container and then quickly set the wick on top. This method is the easiest and fastest, but it's also the least stable, so be careful to not knock the wick out of place as you move on to the next steps.

After you pour in the hot gel, you'll need to make sure that the top of the wick stays centered in the candle. The easiest way to do this is to place two skewers, chopsticks, or pencils in an X shape across the top of the container and prop the wick in one corner to keep it straight as the gel cools. Once the gel is almost cool, gently tug the wick straight.

Set the wick with clear glue, Sticky Wicky, clay, or melted gel, and then prop up the wick with bamboo skewers to keep it straight.

4: melt the gel

Candle gel is usually packaged in a tub of some sort. Tear it out with your fingers or cut it out with a knife or scissors. Melt enough gel to fill the container to the top, less ¼ inch for headroom. You can estimate this amount by eyeballing the container and comparing it to the amount of gel in your melting pot, but if you do, be sure to overestimate. If you underfill the container and then top it off with another batch of melted gel, you will end up with a visible line where the two separate pours meet.

Rather than estimating the quantity of gel you will need for a container, it's better to measure the amount precisely. Simply fill the container with water, stopping ¼ inch from the top. Pour the water into a measuring cup to figure out how much gel you will need. Be sure to dry the container carefully before pouring in the melted gel.

After you determine how much gel you need, cut or tear the gel into small pieces about ½ inch across and put the pieces into the pot. If you drop one large chunk of candle gel into the pot, it will take longer to melt and parts of it will get very hot before other parts have even begun to liquefy. This creates a fire hazard and forces you to stir more frequently. More stirring will create more bubbles in the final candle.

If you are working with direct heat on the stovetop, set the temperature to medium-low. If you are using an enclosed heating device, such as a freestanding electric pot, set the temperature control to 200–225°F. Leave the container uncovered; otherwise, steam will rise to the lid and then condense back down onto the candle gel, resulting in a candle that burns poorly and contains excessive bubbles.

Using a thermometer, heat the gel until it is 190–225°F. How hot you make the gel depends on the density of the gel (see page 38 for guidelines) and on your project. A good general temperature is 200°F. At this temperature, fragrances and colors will blend well. You can heat the gel up to 225°F if you want to reduce the amount bubbles but, for safety, don't exceed 225°F.

Melt small chunks of gel on a hot plate or a stovetop set at a medium-low temperature.

Use measuring spoons or a small dropper to add fragrance to candle gel.

Prepare several color nuggets before you start, so that later you can add small colored pieces to clear gel to achieve the exact shade you want.

5: add fragrance

Add about ½ ounce of fragrance per 16 ounces of candle gel, or 1 tablespoon per 2 cups of gel. If you add too much fragrance oil, you will weaken the gel and make it mushy. Also, completely stir the fragrance into the gel or it will be trapped in the cooled candle as little hot spots of flammable matter, creating a fire hazard. For detailed information on fragrances, see page 27.

6: add color

The uniqueness of candle gel lies in its clarity, so your candle will be beautiful even when it is crystal clear. There are also dyes specifically formulated for use with candle gel. However, most of the candle colorants on the market are made to color traditional opaque candles, which require more dye than transparent candles do in order to achieve a medium shade. While just one drop of concentrated liquid candle color may be fine for a pound of paraffin wax, it can overpower a pound of candle gel.

I strongly suggest that before you begin your adventure into gel candle crafting, you take the time to make up some color nuggets by blending a little colorant with candle gel. You will then be able to tear off pieces of less concentrated color to add to the melting gel. For more information on making color nuggets and working with color, see page 29.

7: position embedments

Candle gel by itself is very pretty. But part of the fun of gel candle crafting is to tell a story or create a montage with various embedments and decorations, such as glass animals, beads, shells, sand, and the like. For more detailed information on what you should or should not embed and how to do it, refer to page 33.

8: pour the gel and let it cool

Do not pour the melted gel all the way to the top of the container. Leave about $1/4$ inch of space between the top of the gel and the top of the container. How you pour the gel into the container determines the amount of bubbles in the finished candle. Think of it like pouring beer or soda into a glass — if you tilt the glass to meet the bottle as you pour, there will be less foam. If you pour the liquid straight from the top, there will be more foam.

In a similar way, if you carefully tilt the container as you pour the gel in, you will reduce the amount of bubbles. If you pour the gel without tilting the container, you will produce more bubbles. For more details about how to create or reduce bubbles, refer to page 36.

Cover the metal tab of the wick with sand, then place heavy embedments at the bottom of the glass. Use fine thread to suspend other embedments and pull the thread out after the gel cools.

Pour the hot gel into the container, being careful not to disturb the wick or the embedments.

Use a heat gun to smooth the surface of the candle and remove blemishes.

9: finish the candle and attach a warning label

Once the candle has fully cooled, trim the wick to ¼ inch. Carefully wipe down the container to remove any spills or fingerprints. Use an oven, a heat gun, a blow dryer, or a heat lamp to polish the surface of the candle and create a more finished appearance. Refer to the heat technique on page 38 for more information.

Don't forget that any candle you give away or sell should come with a warning label. Many people take candles for granted and forget that candles are a small source of fire, and therefore potentially hazardous. Please remind them. An example of a warning label is on page 14.

Let the gel cool, then simply peel it off utensils or out of a container.

10: clean up

Cleaning up is simple if you let the extra bit of melted gel in the pot, the pouring cups, and the other utensils cool. When the gel is cool, you can simply peel it out of a container or off a tool. Put the scraps in a covered container to use in your next project. Then wash all the utensils with soap and water. Some people use the same utensils for cooking later, but I recommend that you dedicate them to candle crafting only.

fire safety

Candle gel is flammable. For your safety, carefully read and follow these tips.

▶ Don't melt the gel over high heat or heat it to more than 225°F. If the gel begins to smoke, it's getting dangerously hot.

▶ If a fire does break out, do not try to put it out with water. Water can make the hot gel splatter and burn your skin. Instead, use a fire extinguisher or smother the flame with a metal pan or lid. Alternatively, throw baking soda on the flame or cover it with a damp cloth.

▶ Never leave melting candle gel unattended. If you are going to be distracted for even a short time, turn the heat off and return to your project when you can be more focused.

▶ If hot candle gel splashes onto your skin, flush it immediately with cold water to reduce the risk of a burn.

▶ Do not pour melted candle gel down the sink. Avoid getting solid bits of candle gel into your drainpipes, too. Candle gel will most definitely cause plumbing problems.

▶ Always attach a warning label to candles that you give away or sell. See page 14 for an example.

Always keep a fire extinguisher, metal lid, box of baking soda, or damp cloth handy.

safety instructions card

The following is an example of the language commonly used in candle warning labels. This is only one example; you may wish to include more detailed recommendations.

warning — candles can cause fires

Please enjoy your candle safely by following these guidelines:

▶ Keep the wick trimmed to $\frac{1}{8}$ to $\frac{1}{4}$ inch high.

▶ Do not allow the candle to burn all the way to the bottom of the container.

▶ Never burn a candle for more than 3 hours at a time.

▶ Keep candles out of the reach of children and pets.

▶ Do not place candles on an unstable surface.

▶ Keep candles away from drapery and other flammable items.

▶ Use common sense and exercise caution.

▶ If your candle has free-floating embedments in it, remove the embedments as the candle burns down and exposes them.

▶ And, remember: *Never leave a burning candle unattended!*

Okay! We've covered the basics of gel candle crafting, and I bet you're eager to get started. Before jumping in, however, take some time to read the important and detailed information in chapter 2. The advice on containers, fragrance, wicks, color, embedments, bubbles, and other waxes will give you the grounding you need to avoid common mistakes and to craft safe, professional-quality candles.

beyond
the basics

As chapter 1 shows, the steps to making gel candles are pretty simple — melt the candle gel, scent it, color it, and pour it into a container prepped with a wick and embedments. If you were casting only a pretty knickknack, you wouldn't need to know much more than the information in chapter 1.

However, you are not making a pretty knickknack. You are making a candle — a functional, combustible item. For this reason, you need a deeper understanding of the types of containers, wicks, fragrances, colors, and waxes that professional gel candle crafters use. By the end of this chapter, you will have the knowledge you need to craft a candle that burns well and is not a safety or fire hazard.

container
concepts

First and foremost, gel candle containers shouldn't be made of flammable materials, such as plastic or wood. The best materials are glass, ceramic, and metal. Glass is the most popular choice, because you can see through it to the beauty of the gel. Polished metal also makes a nice container, since the light of the flame is reflected back up through the gel. The mouth of the container should be wider than or as wide as the bottom of the container, and the overall height should be no greater than 5½ inches.

unique containers

You can buy containers from a candle supply company. It's also fun to recruit a pretty vessel from your home or peruse flea markets for interesting items. Always examine a container for cracks. Some stemware is delicate and cracks when exposed to a flame. Generally, if the item is not dishwasher safe, it should not be used as a candle container.

Glass containers in a wide range of shapes and styles are a popular choice for gel candles, and they give you the opportunity to customize your candles to fit your décor or theme.

container shapes

As a candle burns, it feeds itself with oxygen drawn from the air and with the liquefied gel from the melt pool around the wick. A container of the wrong shape — too tall or too tapered — disrupts this process and causes the flame to die.

For example, imagine that you've fallen into a deep well. The air at the bottom of the well will be stuffy, and it will be difficult to breathe. Eventually, you may run out of breathable air. In a similar way, if you cast a candle into a 12-inch-tall, 1-inch-wide vase, the flame will burn well at first. As the gel melts, the flame will be less able to draw oxygen to survive and will eventually sputter out.

Dramatically tapered containers, such as martini glasses, are also problematic. Imagine that you and a friend are boating on a lake and the boat has a leak. While your friend rows to shore, you bail out water. If the water comes in faster than you can throw it out, the boat will sink. In a similar way, if you cast a candle into a martini glass that is 3 inches wide at the top and ½ inch wide at the base, the candle will burn well at first. As the gel melts, the pool of fuel at the wick's base will become so big that the flame won't be able to burn it up fast enough. Eventually, the flame will be overcome with liquefied gel and drown or make the melt pool burst into flames.

Without special preparation, a martini glass can be a problematic gel candle container.

Just because a container is problematic doesn't mean that you can't use it. You simply have to design around the container's limitations. If your container is made of flammable wood, for instance, you can cast a room fragrancer instead of a candle (see the Room Fragrancer project on page 67). In the case of a tall, narrow vase, you can fill a portion of the container with sand or other nonflammable material to keep the candle portion near the available oxygen (see the Sand Art project on page 71). In the case of a martini glass, you can string glass beads up the wick to snuff out the flame before it burns down to a dangerous level (see the After Six project on page 53).

To use a container that is very tall or sharply tapered, fill the bottom with sand or thread glass beads through the wick so the flame is extinguished before it runs out of air or reaches a large melt pool of liquefied gel at the bottom.

wick wisdom

Candle wicks are available in many sizes and varieties. The preferred wick for a gel candle has the following qualities:

▸ It is made with a zinc-cored or a high-temperature paper (HTP) wick.

▸ It has a metal T-tab at its base that is at least 7/16 inch high.

▸ It has not been heavily preprimed with paraffin.

▸ All of the trapped air in the wick fiber has been removed.

▸ It has been properly sized.

metal-cored and HTP wicks

Gel candle crafters generally prefer to work with zinc-cored wicks. The zinc wire helps the wick stand up straight and makes the flame burn hotter. A hot flame is necessary to burn candle gel, which has a higher melting temperature than traditional waxes. The downside to zinc-cored wicks is that they form tiny "mushrooms" at the top as they burn. These mushrooms must be trimmed off with scissors every now and then.

To avoid unsightly mushrooms, use high-temperature-paper (HTP) wicks, which have no metal core but are designed to burn hot. Since HTP wicks don't stand up straight on their own, they are best used in dense HP candle gel, which will keep the wick upright as it burns.

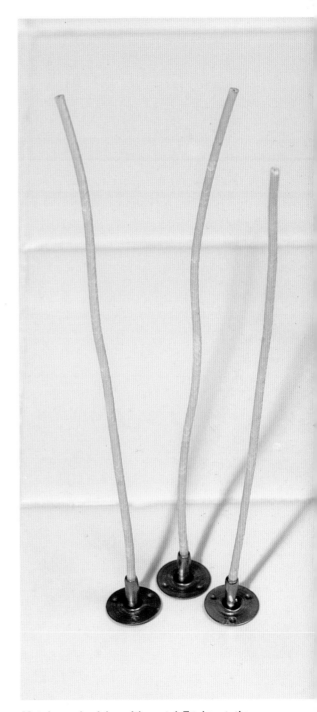

Metal-cored wicks with metal T-tabs at the base are the best choice for gel candles.

metal T-tabs

The importance of metal T-tabs is twofold. First, the tab anchors the end of the wick firmly in place at the bottom of the container. Second, the T portion of the tab snuffs out the flame before it reaches the bottom of the container. If you don't use a self-snuffing wick, the flame will burn all the way to the bottom of the container. When it runs out of wick to burn, it will try to find another source of fuel. Since the flame will be sitting in a pool of melted gel, it will ignite all the liquid at once and turn the candle into a fireball.

Not only must you use a T-tabbed wick, but you must also make sure that the T is at least $7/16$ inch tall. Most T-tabbed wicks in craft stores are designed for use in traditional wax candles, which call for a much shorter T. Since candle gel burns at a higher temperature than traditional waxes, it must be snuffed out at least $7/16$ inch above the bottom of the container. If the tab is not tall enough, thread glass, ceramic, or metal beads along the wick to attain the proper height. The beads will act like the metal tab and snuff out the flame before it reaches a dangerous level.

preprimed wicks

If you purchase wicks that are specifically designed for candle gel, you can set them without any further preparation. However, since gel candle crafting is a relatively new hobby, most wicks on the market are still designed for paraffin and other opaque waxes. Such wicks are preprimed with paraffin wax to ensure that they burn well. You can tell whether a wick is preprimed by running your fingernail along it. If it feels waxy or if your nail removes a waxy coat, the wick has been primed with paraffin.

The wax on most preprimed wicks melts at about 140–145°F. When you pour hot candle gel over the wick, the paraffin starts to melt off, which creates a tornado of cloudiness in the middle of the candle that is impossible to remove. One solution to this problem is to use a wick that has been preprimed with a wax that melts at 212°F, and then to pour the candle gel at a lower temperature. Alternatively, you can melt off the paraffin wax by placing the wick on a thick piece of paper towel and warming it in the oven at 220°F for 15 minutes. Check the wick frequently to make sure it doesn't turn brown.

You can either leave the metal tab exposed at the base of the candle or cover it up with sand or embedments.

air in the wicking

Wicks are made of either cotton or paper, so air gets trapped in between the fibers. This is not important when you are casting a candle with an opaque wax. However, when the air escapes into transparent candle gel, it creates tiny bubbles that can ruin your design.

One solution is to purchase wick that has been especially kneaded by heavy machinery to remove all of the air before it is primed. Another solution is to use the heat technique (see page 38) to remove air bubbles later.

my tried-and-true method

My own method for dealing with preprimed wick and entrapped air is to cook the wicks in melted candle gel before I set them in the containers. Here's how to do this:

1. In a pot, melt a small amount of clear gel to approximately 220°F.

2. Drop the wick in the melted gel. It will immediately bubble, and you will see the paraffin melt off.

3. When all the paraffin has melted off and the entrapped air has escaped (about a minute), grab the tab portion of the wick with a pair of chopsticks or a fork and remove it from the pot.

4. Set the chopsticks or the fork on the countertop so that the wick hangs over the edge of the counter toward the floor.

5. As the wick cools, tug it straight.

If you use this technique, be careful that the wick doesn't get too hot or it will start to turn brown. This will not affect the wick's ability to burn, but it may ruin your design.

Most wicks have air trapped inside the fibers, which creates tiny bubbles in gel candles. You can either remove the air from the wick before casting the candle or use the heat technique to remove the bubbles after casting the candle.

wick sizes

A wick is labeled according to the size of candle it is designed to burn. The bigger the candle, the larger the wick. If you are purchasing wicks from gel candle suppliers, they will correctly identify the wick as a small, medium, or large gel candle wick (see the chart below). However, general craft suppliers may make no distinction between wicks for traditional waxes and those for candle gel.

Since candle gel burns hotter than traditional waxes, the wick should be one size larger than that used for a regular candle. Use the following chart to help you select the right size wick.

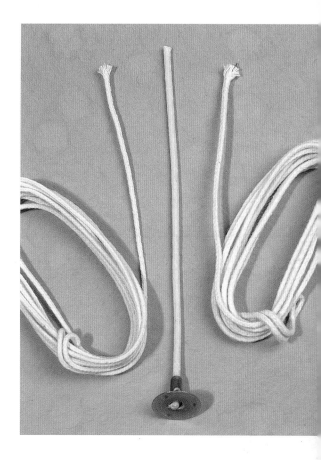

Wick comes in a range of sizes, including medium and large, shown here.

what it says on the label	what it means to a traditional candle crafter	what it means to a gel candle crafter
Small	1- to 1¾-inch-diameter containers (e.g., votive holder)	Don't use this wick
Medium	2- to 2½-inch-diameter containers (e.g., jelly jar)	Use this wick for 1- to 1¾-inch-diameter containers (e.g., votive holder)
Large	3- to 3¼-inch-diameter containers (e.g. coffee mug)	Use this wick for 2- to 2½-inch-diameter containers (e.g., jelly jar)
Extra large	3½- to 5-inch-diameter containers (e.g., apothecary jar)	Use this wick for 3- to 3¼-inch-diameter containers (e.g., coffee mug)

For containers that are more than 3¼ inches wide, you will have to use more than one wick (see Multiwicks on page 26).

multiwicks

If your container is unusually large, you are better off using multiwicks — two or more wicks in the same candle. To use two wicks, mark the middle of the container and then place one wick in the center of each of the resulting halves. To use three wicks, divide the container into thirds.

In any case, make sure that you size the wick correctly. For example, if you have a 6-inch-diameter container, divide it into two 3-inch sections and place a wick in each section that is appropriate for a 3-inch candle. Always keep the number to no more than five wicks per candle.

Large containers need two or more wicks in order to burn correctly.

fragrance facts

The type of fragrance you use to scent your candle is very important — you can't use just anything. The fragrance must meet three criteria: strength, flash-point safety, and solubility.

strength

Most fragrance oils manufactured for candles smell very strong. This strength ensures that when the candle burns it "throws" enough fragrance. If you use weak fragrance oils, you will be disappointed and you may add more fragrance than you should. Too much fragrance oil creates a fire hazard, weakens the candle gel, and causes cloudiness. If you purchase fragrance oils that are manufactured specifically for candlemaking, the strength should be adequate. For LP gel, use ¼ to ½ ounce of fragrance per pound of candle gel. For MP gel, use ½ to ¾ ounce of fragrance per pound of gel. And for HP gel, use up to 1 ounce of fragrance per pound of gel.

A variety of synthetic fragrance oils can be used to scent gel candles.

flash-point safety

Flash point is the temperature at which fragrance vapors ignite in the presence of a spark. Candle fragrance oils usually have flash points between 140° and 220°F. Candle gel manufacturers recommend using fragrances with flash points of 170°F or higher. Therefore, even if your fragrance works for traditional candles, its flashpoint may be too low for gel candles. Always doube check the flashpoint with your supplier.

solubility

Fragrance oils are made from a number of ingredients, some of which are not soluble in mineral oil, the primary ingredient in candle gel. Such fragrances may separate out completely, either above or below the gel, resulting in a hazardous pool of flammable oil. Or they may only partly dissolve and make the candle cloudy.

You can test for solubility by shaking 1 part fragrance oil in 3 parts ordinary mineral or baby oil. Allow the mixture to stand for 5 minutes. If the fragrance oil is nonsoluble, it will separate from the mineral or baby oil just like oil separates from water. Another way to test for solubility is to make a small trial candle. You may waste some material, but you will know for sure whether the fragrance oil will work in your candle.

With the primary colors of yellow, red, and blue, you can blend a variety of unique hues.

color
cool

Adding color to gel candles raises three important issues: blending colors, dealing with bleeding, and understanding the effect of the gel's transparency on color.

blending colors

Try to find candle colorants formulated for candle gel. Most candle colorants formulated for traditional waxes are quite concentrated. For example, 3 drops of concentrated candle colorant will tint 1 pound of paraffin wax to a medium shade. Since paraffin wax is naturally opaque, it requires more color to reach a medium shade than transparent candle gel does. Therefore, only 1 or 2 drops of liquid dye can usually tint 1 pound of candle gel to a medium shade. If you want to create a single shade, such as red, this is not a problem. But if you are trying to blend your own shade of red, a color that uses a little red, a little orange, and a tad of black, you will very quickly stumble onto the problem of either overcoloring your gel or of coloring more gel than you really meant to.

For this reason, I recommend that you premix a small amount of candle gel in the colors that you want to work with, and then tear off bits of the precolored gel and melt it along with uncolored gel. By doing this, you will dilute the colorant and have more control over the shade of gel you produce.

If you have an understanding of color theory and color blending, you can take this idea a step further by predyeing red, blue, yellow, and black candle gel and then using these gels on a project-by-project basis. To do this, melt 4 ounces of candle gel and color it with 4 drops of candle dye. Pour the gel into a container and allow it to cool. For the black gel, you may wish to melt only 2 ounces of candle gel with 2 drops of dye, as you will tend to use less of this color in your blends.

As you craft your candles, tear off pea-sized pieces of the precolored gel into the melting pot. Slowly build the color up to the hue and intensity that you want. Because your melting pot is likely to be made of metal, it will be difficult to see the exact color you have achieved unless you spoon out a sample of the melted gel and pour it onto a white cutting board or plate. When the sample cools, you can peel it up and examine it in the light.

recreating colors

Color blending is a meditative and challenging part of the candlemaking process. I like to compare it to seasoning a pot of soup, sampling and tasting and adding a pinch of this or that along the way until it is just right. You may wish to keep notes so that you can recreate a color later (for example, "this orange color was achieved with 2 pea-sized pieces of red and 1 pea-sized piece of yellow in 1 cup of clear gel").

To test gel candle colors, pour onto a white plate and let cool, then hold up to the light.

color bleeding

Candle colors bleed. This means that if you place red-colored gel shaped like apples in a light-green candle, over time the red dye will leach out and stain the surrounding gel. Eventually, it will be difficult to tell that you started out with apple shapes. Instead, they will look like red blobs.

Bleeding is a fact of life for the gel candle crafter, so if you are developing a design, you must accept the bleeding and design around it. Here are some ways to do that.

▸ Use designs that will look beautiful after the colors bleed and don't try to force clear, distinct lines between colors (see the Rainbow candle, page 75).

▸ Instead of embedding a shaped design made from candle gel, embed something else to achieve the look you want. For example, embed a piece of blue clay or a blue bead rather than a square of blue gel.

▸ Keep your colors light. The more dye you use, the more bleeding there will be.

▸ Surround colored gel with other types of waxes, which will prevent the dye from bleeding so readily (see the Stars and Dreidels Project, page 95).

The dyes in candle gel tend to bleed over time and create fuzzy lines. The red blobs in this candle were once distinct apple shapes.

transparency and color

If you use more than one color in your candle project, you need to pay special attention to how those colors will look together, since the gel's transparency makes them blend visually. For example, say you have two pieces of colored glass; one is red and one is blue. If you stack the red piece in front of the blue or vice versa, you will see purple.

Now imagine that you have made a gel candle that is red on the bottom and blue on the top. If you place the candle at eye level and look at it, you will see the two colors quite distinctly. But usually when we look at a candle we do not look at it straight on. In fact, usually we look down on a candle. If you look down on your red and blue candle, you will see purple.

This blending together of colors in a candle is very cool! But, rather quickly, you can run into problems. Suppose that instead of using red and blue, you get into the holiday spirit and create a red and green candle. Unfortunately, red and green blend to make muddy brown. Therefore, when you look down on a red and green candle, you will see brown.

tips for transparent color

There is no "solution" to the way in which transparency affects color, it's just one of those things you learn to think about. Here are some tips to keep in mind as you craft your candles.

▶ Consider using clear gel or just one color of gel.

▶ If you decide to make stripes, consider going from a dark color at the bottom of the container to a light color on the top. A dark color on the top will make the colors underneath impossible to see.

▶ Do not use too many colors in one candle. I prefer to use no more than three colors at one time.

▶ Use opaque waxes, such as paraffin, to halt transparency and create a break between colors so that they don't visually blend together.

Gel's transparency make the clear, lavender, and turquoise colors in this candle blend together visually.

embedment
embellishment

The unique transparency and viscosity of candle gel take it beyond its primary use as a candle material and give it a secondary life as a marvelous casting medium. Once you get started in gel candle crafting, all sorts of decorative bric-a-brac suddenly seem just right for cobbling up your latest thematic montage. Unfortunately, creativity often rushes in front of practicality and safety. The bottom line is that not everything is appropriate for embedding in a gel candle. It's important to consider the material the embedment is made from and whether it is safe to use in a burning candle.

safe materials

The basic rule for embedments is not to use flammable materials. Here are examples of materials that are safe to embed in a gel candle.

- Aluminum foil
- Ceramic beads
- Clay sculptures
- Glass beads*
- Glitter
- Gold leaf
- Metal coins
- Mirrors
- Salt, sand, and gravel (the salt should not contain dextrose)
- Shells and rocks
- Wax (beeswax, paraffin, or other waxes)

* Some plastics and resins look an awful lot like glass. To make sure that an embedment is made of glass, tap it sharply against a glass surface. The embedment should ring out rather than make a dull thud. If it thuds, it is probably made from plastic or resin.

A sampling of items that are safe to embed in candle gel includes glass marbles, shells, metal, stones, and sea glass.

unsafe materials

Here are some examples of things that are NOT safe to embed in a gel candle, because they are flammable or because they melt, rot, or emit a noxious odor.

- ▶ Candy or anything with sugar
- ▶ Dried herbs
- ▶ Dried starfish and seahorses
- ▶ Paper
- ▶ Plastic toys
- ▶ Rubber erasers
- ▶ Wooden beads

safe use of flammables

Just because something is not appropriate to embed in a gel candle does not mean that you can't find ways to work with it. Here are some ways in which you could incorporate flammable items into your candle design without compromising safety.

- ▶ Use hot glue or decoupage techniques to affix the item to the outside of the container. For instance, a decoupage of a dried pansy on the outside of a container can be just as pretty as a dried pansy embedded inside the candle.
- ▶ Design your candle so that it snuffs itself out at least ½ inch above the flammable material. See the Botanical Bounty project on page 83 as an example.
- ▶ Use the embedment as a decorative element near the candle or in its packaging.
- ▶ Don't put a wick in the candle gel; turn the project into a scent bowl instead. See the Room Fragrancer project on page 67.
- ▶ Nest the candle container inside a larger container and place the embedments in the gap between the two. See the Pasta Fiesta project on page 117.

Dried flowers, wooden blocks, plastic items, and candy are not safe to embed in candle gel unless they are placed well below where the wick will burn.

placement

It's important to plan where and how you'll place embedments in the candle gel. For example, if you are putting a glass fish into a fishbowl candle, you want the fish to look like it is happily swimming around the middle of the bowl. You do not want it lying flat on its side at the bottom of the basin. Embedments have weight, and if you drop them into the cooling gel, they will eventually find their way to the bottom of the container. Here are some techniques to make sure that embedments stay exactly where you want them.

▸ Affix the embedments to the inside of the container wall with fast-setting clear epoxy glue.

▸ Attach the embedments to each other with fast-setting clear epoxy glue. For example, glue the glass fish to a shell, then let the shell settle to the bottom of the container. The fish will appear to be swimming just above the shell.

▸ Suspend the embedments in place with a very fine thread or wire. For instance, if you want to embed a small ornament that has a hole in the top, loop a thread through the hole, tie the thread to a skewer, then rest the skewer on the lip of the container while the gel cools. Later, when you pull the thread out of the gel, it will leave very little trace.

One way to position embedments is to attach them to each other with clear glue before placing them in the candle container.

However you affix the embedments, remember that if they are not made of gel or wax, then they must be out of the way of the wick. If, for example, you put a seashell right up against the wick, then when the flame burns down to that point, it will likely be snuffed out. You should place non-wax embedments close to the interior wall of the container and out of the way of the wick.

bubble basics

First of all, let me say loud and clear: Bubbles are not imperfections. In fact, the sooner that you learn to love each and every wonderful bubble in your gel candles, the sooner you will become a very happy gel candle crafter. Bubbles are what make gel candles so lovely to look at when they are not burning and even more so when they are.

As you advance in gel candle crafting, however, it's helpful to understand "bubble control." Sometimes you will want lots of bubbles, as in a frothy beer candle, for example. Other times you will want no bubbles, perhaps for a candle meant to look like burgundy wine. Occasionally, you will want just enough bubbles, such as a seascape with bubbles surrounding embedments but not obscuring them.

What are bubbles, anyway? Basically, bubbles are the result of air trapped inside the candle gel trying to get out. To prevent bubbles, you should focus on two things. First, avoid getting air in the gel in the first place and, second, give any trapped air plenty of time to escape.

don't trap air in the gel

Trapping air in candle gel is a relatively common problem for those new to the craft. Here are some typical situations that introduce air into gel candles.

▸ Is there any water in the gel? If your melting pot and utensils are wet, the water will evaporate off as the gel heats up. This evaporation will rise up through the gel as bubbles.

▸ Are you covering the pot while you melt the gel? As the gel heats up, it turns the air above it into steam. If you cover the pot, the steam will condense on the lid and then fall back into the gel, creating bubbles.

▸ How are you stirring in the fragrance and color? Fast, rapid strokes will introduce air into the gel. Stir slowly and evenly.

▸ Have you prepped the wick to remove paraffin wax and air? See page 24 for information on removing air from wicks.

▸ Do your embedments have undercuts and air pockets? For example, look at a seashell's curves and holes. When you pour gel around it, air is trapped inside the shell. To solve this problem, dip the embedment in candle gel and allow it to cool. Make sure all holes and gaps are filled. Or you can fill the holes and gaps with fast-setting clear epoxy glue.

► How are you pouring the gel into the containers? Think of a bartender pouring a glass of beer. The bartender tips the glass to meet the neck of the beer bottle or tap and lets the beer run along the side of the glass. Similarly, if you tilt the container to meet the pouring spout — or carefully ladle the gel into the container — you will reduce bubbles.

give trapped air time to escape

If you do introduce air into the gel, you can coax it out by giving it plenty of time to escape. Here are some suggestions.

► What type of gel are you working with? HP gel solidifies more quickly than LP gel does. As a result, HP gel tends to have more bubbles.

► How hot is the gel when you pour it into the container? The hotter the candle gel is, the more liquid it becomes, and the more time the bubbles have to escape.

► When are you stirring in the fragrance and the color? To reduce bubbles, add the fragrance and the color at a temperature of 210–215°F. At this temperature, the gel is more fluid and you don't need to stir it as much.

► How hot is the gel when you pour it into the container? Pouring at a temperature of 210–215°F will ensure fewer bubbles, since the gel is more fluid and any trapped air can escape more easily.

► Is the container cold when you pour the hot gel into it? If so, the gel will cool

rapidly, decreasing the amount of time in which bubbles can escape. To avoid this, warm the empty container in an oven or a hot-water bath before pouring hot gel into it.

► Are you tapping the sides and bottom of the container? After pouring the candle gel, tap the outside of the container to encourage the trapped air to start its journey up and out of the candle gel.

► How fast does the gel cool in the container? The slower the cooling time, the greater the opportunity for trapped air to escape. You can slow down the cooling process by placing the container in a hot-water bath while the gel cools. Or you can use the heat technique to slow the cooling phase.

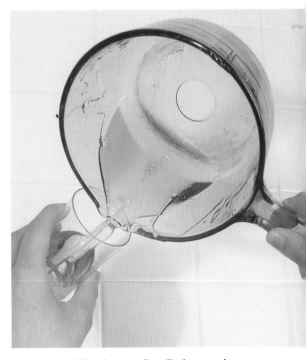

To reduce bubbles in a candle, tilt the container and pour the gel along the side of the glass.

the heat technique

The heat technique is the process of rewarming the candle gel with a heat gun, in an oven, or with a heat lamp to reduce or eliminate bubbles, lines formed from a multiple pour, or surface imperfections caused by finger pokes and the like. It is often the final step in the candlemaking process. However, do not use the heat technique under the following conditions:

▶ If your candle contains wax embedments or colored chunks of gel. The heat will melt these embedments, causing them to fall out of place, lose their shape, or melt into the surrounding gel.

▶ If you have embedded anything in the candle without first gluing it in place. In this case, the embedment will fall out of suspension as the gel liquefies and will end up at the bottom of the container. See page 35 for tips on gluing embedments.

▶ If you are not willing to monitor and focus on your project throughout the process. Placing a flammable candle into a hot oven or near a heat lamp is a fire hazard. I can tell you from personal experience that it is extremely agonizing — as well as inexcusable — to be 20 miles away from home and suddenly remember that you left a candle melting in a gas oven! Also, after you reheat the gel, the wick will most likely have wandered off center and you'll need to keep an eye on the candle during its cooling phase and regularly tug the wick straight.

You can use a heat gun, an oven, or heat lamps, for the heat technique. The pros and cons of each and how to use them are discussed next.

using a heat gun

A heat gun or a hair dryer is the best tool for fixing spot problems, such as imperfections caused by finger pokes. Unlike the oven, which heats the entire candle evenly, the heat gun can be aimed directly at the problem area. As you use a heat gun, keep an eye out for hot spots that can lead to container cracks.

Surface bubbles (above) can be diminished with a heat gun for a more finished look (below).

using an oven

Set the temperature to 220°F and place the candle on a cookie sheet in the middle of a clean oven. Check the candle every 15 minutes or so. When you are satisfied, turn off the oven but leave the candle inside so that it cools to room temperature as slowly as possible. It is not uncommon for this method to take as long as an hour. The oven is the best method for getting rid of bubbles. It is not recommended for smoothing out lines between color pours because the oven will melt the separate pours into one single color.

using heat lamps

Place a couple of heat lamps or light fixtures with 60-watt lightbulbs about 3 inches away from the sides of the candle container. Check the temperature of the container frequently to make sure that hot spots aren't developing, which can cause the container to crack.

It is also a good idea to rotate the container periodically, so that the heat is evenly dispersed over the candle. The heat lamp method is especially good for smoothing out the lines that sometimes appear between two or more pours of the same color.

This candle was not treated with the heat technique and has bubbles as part of the design.

This candle was treated with the heat technique to produce a more bubble-free seascape.

wax whimsy

Of all the crafts that I have embraced, making candles out of traditional waxes, such as paraffin and beeswax, has not been one of them. I enjoy traditional wax candles, but I just hate the mess. I was so relieved to discover easy-to-clean candle gel that I never thought a time would come when I would dig out my old melting pots and work with traditional wax again.

However, as I experimented more and more with candle gel, I became curious about how traditional waxes could be incorporated into my projects. I have since found that the opacity of traditional wax makes it an excellent visual barrier between and around transparent candle gel. One such example is the Stars and Dreidels project on page 95.

In addition, because traditional waxes are hard, they make excellent containers for candle gel. Several projects in chapter 5 show examples of how to do this. However, the most common use for traditional waxes in gel candle projects is as embedments. The Citrus Slices and Fruit Preserves projects on pages 99 and 101, respectively, are examples of this. The following chart includes types of waxes and how they can be used in gel candle crafting.

wax	approximate melting point	attributes
Low melt-point (MP) paraffin, soft wax, and one-pour wax	130°F or less	Recommended for hand-sculpted embedments (see Citrus Slices on page 99) or as a backdrop to transparent gel (see Stars and Dreidels on page 95)
Medium MP paraffin and votive wax	130–145°F	General purpose wax usually found in craft stores; recommended for creating containers (see Sunflower Surprise and Red, White, and Blue on pages 91 and 105, respectively)
High MP paraffin, pillar wax, and votive wax	145–150°F	Recommended for casting embedments (see Fruit Preserves on page 101)
Beeswax	150°F	Recommended for creating containers (see Honey Pot on page 103) or for softening votive wax used for containers (see Red, White, and Blue on page 105)

If you have any familiarity with traditional waxes, you probably have the equipment and knowledge you need to start experimenting on your own. If you have never used them, please read an introductory book on the craft or ask your vendor questions before beginning a project that involves wax casting. If you would like to embed wax shapes in your candle but don't want to cast them yourself, several vendors listed in the Appendix sell premade wax embedments at very reasonable prices (see page 134).

That's the whole ball of wax — or gel, I should say. Since experience is the best teacher, it's time for you to jump in and start crafting. The projects that follow are based on the 10 Easy Steps covered in chapter 1. Where instructions vary, I've included some tips.

Chapter 3 shows you how to make simple gel candle projects that require little in the way of special techniques or added goodies. Next, chapter 4 teaches you how to make and work with embedments so that you can create your own thematic projects. Chapter 5 suggests some special effects you can create by blending the gel with traditional candle waxes. Finally, chapter 6 shows you how to design and decorate various containers to make your candles especially unique.

packaging gel candles

There are two important things to consider when packaging gel candles. First, protect the top surface from finger pokes. You can do this easily by purchasing premade plastic covers from the vendors listed on page 134 or by making your own. Second, include a set of safety instructions (see the sample on page 14).

In terms of decorative packaging, don't overdo it. A simple ribbon tied around the container looks perfectly fine. Some clear or decorative cellophane tied over the top of the candle can also add interest. Beyond that, let the candles speak for themselves.

Clear cellophane and a ribbon make simple but decorative packaging.

simple
projects

Whether you are whipping up a few simple votive candles for a casual dinner party or preparing keepsake hostess gifts for your child's wedding, the projects that follow are guaranteed to be fast, easy, and fun.

Bubbles, abundant and fat, will glimmer and shimmer. Swirling colors will entice and delight. Fragrances will waft. Beauty will be your goal, and a panoply of appreciative *oohs* and *aahs* will be your reward. All this, and in only an hour or so of your time!

cut-glass candles

Single-pour gel candles are very quick and easy to make. It takes only an hour or less to create a batch to coordinate with your tablecloth, dinnerware, or party décor. For this project, use cut-glass votive holders or an assortment of other cut- or pressed-glass containers scavenged from your kitchen cupboards, such as ashtrays, salt cellars, jam jars, and the like. While gel candles are perfectly lovely in clear glass, cut- or pressed-glass containers add extra complexity to candlelight.

what you will learn:

How to use gel candles as a color-coordinated (and temporary) accent to your décor.

special materials:

► assortment of cut- or pressed-glass containers

► candle colorant(s) to match your décor

SETTING THE WICK

Don't glue the wick to the container. These are temporary candles, so you want to be able to remove the gel and the wick at the end of the evening and place the containers back on the shelves. Instead, pour a little melted gel into the container and then immediately set the wick. After it is completely cool, fill the rest of the container. Since you are casting into cut-glass containers, no one will see the line that forms between the two pours.

COLORING THE CANDLES

Dye the gel to match your décor. If you plan to use the candles on the table, don't scent them, since the aroma may over-whelm the smell of the food.

CLEANING UP

When the festivities are over, allow the remaining candle gel to cool. Turn the candle upside down and snip off any charred wick (if you turn it upside down first, the charred wick will not fall onto the sticky gel). Scoop the gel out of the container with your fingers. Remove the wicks by pulling them out from the bottom. Set the gel and wicks aside to reuse in another candle project. Wash the containers with soap and water and put them away until your next party.

toasting the bride
and groom

Candle gel naturally makes a lot of cheerful bubbles, so creating candles that look like champagne is as easy as popping open a bottle of bubbly. Arrange the finished candles on top of a mirrored or silver charger to reflect their brilliance when they burn. Since your guests are bound to admire their beauty, make some extras to give away as memorable party gifts.

what you will learn:

How candle gel naturally makes lots of bubbles.

special materials:

- ► clear champagne glasses
- ► salt, sand, or a few glass, ceramic or metal beads (the salt should not contain dextrose)
- ► champagne fragrance oil or other scent
- ► colorants that look like champagne or match your décor (optional)
- ► packaging materials, such as cellophane and ribbon (optional)

SETTING THE WICK

Don't glue the wick to the container. These are temporary candles, so you want to be able to remove the wick at the end of the evening. Instead, pour a little melted gel into the container and immediately set the wick. Let it cool.

COVERING THE TAB

After the wick has set, pour about a tablespoon of salt or sand over the metal tab to cover it up. Alternatively, string glass, ceramic, or metal beads on the wick to hide the metal tab.

MAKING THE CANDLE

Add the fragrance oil to the melted gel. Color the gel to look like champagne or to match your décor, if desired. Let the gel cool slightly, then pour it from high above the glass. This technique makes lots of bubbles. If you want, stir the top a little with a metal spoon to make it even frothier.

CREATING PARTY FAVORS

If you want, wrap some candles to give away as keepsake gifts (see page 41 for packaging ideas).

color
collection

This project is a fun way to experiment with color to achieve just the shades you want. The clean lines of the glass and the relatively bubble-free gel make these candles stunning in their elegant simplicity.

what you will learn:

How to blend complex colors.

special materials:

▶ red, yellow, and blue colorants

▶ 3 glass bowls or pitchers

▶ containers with clean lines

CREATING COLOR CHUNKS

Melt some clear gel and dye it with the red, yellow, and blue colorants in three separate batches. Pour each batch into a bowl and let them cool.

BLENDING COLORS

Melt some more clear gel and add small pieces of red and blue color chunks to make purple, red and yellow to make orange, and yellow and blue to make green. Experiment with various shades, adding more or less of each color and more or less clear gel. Spoon small samples onto a white plate or another flat surface. Let the gel cool, peel it off the plate and hold it up to the light to check the color. When you are satisfied with the color, pour the candle. Use simple containers to show off your unique color blends.

A beautiful shade of periwinkle is accented with beads in matching tones.

WORLD FAMOUS EGG CREAM

Junior's

BERRY OR   u-bet   COFFEE SYRUP

soda fountain

Some of us may remember the treat of a big, frothy soft drink at the corner soda fountain. For others, this candle is a symbolic remembrance of times gone by. This project will show you that there are numerous ways to fool the eye and delight the spirit when crafting with candle gel.

what you will learn:

How to make carbonation foam.

special materials:

▸ containers that match the type of drink you wish to make
▸ fragrance oils, such as root beer, cola, strawberry, and champagne.
▸ colorants that match your drink theme
▸ 2 ounces paraffin wax or 1-inch tall scrap of white candle
▸ double boiler (see right for an inexpensive, temporary setup)
▸ old fork

CREATING A THEME

Select containers, fragrance oils, and colorants that create a drink theme.

MAKING CARBONATION FOAM

To make carbonation foam for frothy drinks, let the gel cool completely. This should take about 3 hours. Melt paraffin or a candle scrap in a double boiler. If you use a scrap candle, fish out the old wick and throw it away. As the paraffin cools, whip it with a fork. When it begins to clump, spread it on top of the candle gel. Poke and prod the wax with the fork.

an easy double boiler

The problem with traditional waxes is that whatever you melt them in is difficult to clean out. Rather than using your good pots for melting wax, use two old coffee cans or similar metal containers, one larger than the other. Melt the wax in the smaller can set inside the larger can filled with water. Gently heat both cans on the stovetop until the wax is melted. When finished, simply toss the waxy metal can into the garbage.

after six

This project is a fun way to use interesting glasses with classic shapes. Glass swizzle sticks, which add a nice retro flair, are available in unique and eclectic designs. This project uses martini glasses, but you can make drink-theme candles in wine, margarita, and cocktail glasses, as well. Follow the 10 Easy Steps on page 7 with these variations.

what you will learn:
How to use a container with a narrow base.

special materials:
- glass beads with a hole wide enough for the wick to pass through
- fragrance oils that are appropriate to a drink theme
- colorants
- martini glasses (can substitute with wine, margarita, or cocktail glasses)

A glass swizzle stick with a glass olive makes the perfect accessory for this gel martini.

POURING A MARTINI
When using martini, margarita, and other types of glasses with narrow bases, string glass beads along the wick so the gel doesn't burn down to the bottom and become a fire hazard (see page 19 for more information). Scent and color the candle gel. Set the swizzle stick in the glass, then pour in the gel.

MAKING WINE AND MARGARITAS
For wine, margaritas, and other drinks that have no natural carbonation, remove bubbles from the gel with the heat technique (see page 38). To finish off a margarita, wait until the candle is completely cool. Then, run a thin bead of glue around the rim of the glass and immediately dip it into a plate of salt.

stripe
hype

There are many interesting ways you can layer candle gel to achieve a unique design. The first layer should be the darkest shade, as you will be looking down into the candle and don't want dark gel to obscure the colors beneath it. For a more interesting design, experiment with making the layers different heights rather than uniform stripes.

what you will learn:
How to layer candle gel.

special materials:
▸ candle colorants
▸ simple container

This striped candle is an effective design because the bottom colors are close in tone while the top color provides a sharp contrast.

POURING THE FIRST STRIPE
Melt some clear gel and dye it to make the first layer. Pour it into a prepared container and let it cool completely.

POURING THE SECOND STRIPE
Melt and dye the next layer of gel, making sure it is a lighter shade than the first. When the first layer is cool, pour the second layer.

POURING THE LAST STRIPE
Melt and dye the last layer of gel, making sure it is a lighter shade than the layers beneath it. When the second layer is cool, pour the third stripe.

valentine's day

The only thing more romantic than an aromatic candle shaped like a heart is a candle that has been specially hand-crafted for a loved one.

This project gives you an excuse to practice temperature control in order to achieve a two-toned candle. If you pour the colors when they are too hot, they will just run together. If you pour the colors when they are too cold, they will sit on either side of the wick like blobs. You could smooth them out using the heat technique (see page 38), but you'll produce a better candle if you learn how to pour the two colors just right.

what you will learn:
How to make a two-pour gel candle.

special materials:
- aphrodisiac fragrances
- red candle colorant
- 2 pouring pitchers
- heart-shaped container
- glitter

CREATING TWO SHADES
Melt the gel, then add the aphrodisiac fragrance and a small amount of red candle colorant to create a light red shade. Pour equal amounts of the melted gel into two separate pouring pitchers (glass pitchers work well because you can see the colors). Add more of the red colorant to one of the pitchers to create a dark red shade.

POURING THE CANDLE
When the gel has cooled to approximately 190°F, position yourself over the container and hold a pouring pitcher in each hand. Pour in the two colors simultaneously. It's important that the gel be sufficiently cool, or the colors will just run together.

ADDING THE GLITTER
Add a sprinkle of very finely cut glitter to the top of the candle. When the candle burns, not only does it smell enticing, but the glitter also gives the flame a little extra liveliness that is simply mesmerizing to watch.

ocean
waves

It's amazing the range of hues you can create to give the effect of ocean waves. This project shows you how to play with similar ranges of colored gel, layering the shades at various angles to create a unique design. Since candle gel tends to bleed over time, the layers will become less and less distinct, forming a lovely design.

what you will learn:
How to layer candle gel at various angles.

special materials:
▶ clear containers
▶ colorants

POURING THE FIRST LAYER

Melt, scent, and color all of the gel you'll need for this project. I used turquoise, seafoam green, and aqua shades, making each layer progressively lighter in tone. Tip the container slightly and prop it in position. Pour the first layer of gel into the container. The gel will harden at a bit of an angle. Let it cool completely. The container must be cool to the touch, or the angle of the gel will not set and eventually turn into a horizontal line.

POURING THE SECOND LAYER

When the first pour has cooled and hardened, reheat the next layer of gel, making sure it is a lighter shade. Tip the container slightly in the other direction and prop it up. Pour the second layer into the container and let it cool completely.

POURING THE THIRD LAYER

Melt the last layer of gel, making sure it is an even lighter shade. Don't tip the container in this step, so that the last layer hardens in a horizontal line. Pour in the remaining gel and let it cool.

Even something as simple as bath beads in fun shapes and iridescent colors can provide a nice external decorative element.

swirl
twirl

Here's another way to use candle colorant to achieve a fun design. Rather than adding dye to the melted gel, you add a few drops to clear, melted gel that has already been poured into the container. When you twirl the container around by the stem, the dye forms intensely colored swirls against a clear background. Experiment and see what you can create.

what you will learn:
How to swirl color into a candle.

special materials:
- ▶ container
- ▶ toothpick
- ▶ liquid candle colorant
- ▶ oven mitts

POURING CLEAR GEL

Heat uncolored gel to 200°F and pour it into a prepared container. A container with a stem (such as a wine glass) works well for easy twirling.

SWIRLING THE DESIGN

Using a toothpick, place four small dots of concentrated liquid candle colorant at the north, south, east, and west points of the gel. Quickly twirl the glass in your hand to make the colorant swirl into the gel (wear oven mitts, as the glass will be hot). You can also twirl the wick to make a spiral design. Place the candle in the refrigerator to set the gel quickly and preserve your design.

At first, colored swirls are very vivid, but after a few days the dye blends into the rest of the gel and forms a more subtle design, shown at right.

Jell-O parfait

One day as I was browsing the used bookstore shelves, I stumbled upon a tiny pamphlet written in the 1950s that was dedicated to preparing, crafting, and otherwise having fun with Jell-O. Within 15 seconds it clicked: Candle gel looks like Jello-O, feels like Jello-O, and can be made to smell like Jello-O . . . oh my! (Before beginning, you may want to tie a smart little apron around your cinched day dress and give your hair a little flip.)

what you will learn:
How to use the chunks technique.

special materials:
- fragrance oils with fruit scents
- candle colorants in light, bright colors
- small cookie sheet, shallow bowl, or other temporary sheet mold
- dessert container
- approximately 2 ounces paraffin wax or 1-inch of a white scrap candle to make whipped cream (optional)

MAKING JELL-O CHUNKS
Premake chunks of scented, colored Jell-O by dyeing some gel a light, bright color, and then pouring it into a small, shallow sheet mold until the gel is approximately an inch thick. Allow it to cool completely, then peel it up. Cut the gel into squares with scissors. Place the chunks around the wick in a dessert container. Heat a small amount of clear, scented gel to 180°F and pour it over the top to "glue" the chunks in place.

MAKING WHIPPED CREAM
To make Jell-O with whipped cream, place the chunks inside the container and heat a small amount of light-colored gel to 180°F. Pour the gel around the chunks. Layer a bit of melted paraffin "foam" in the manner described in the Soda Fountain project on page 51. This layer can go on top of the chunks or in between gel layers. Since candle gel has a higher melting point than paraffin, the hot paraffin will not melt the gel chunks.

MAKING AMBROSIA
To make Jell-O ambrosia, make a sheet of precolored gel using the method described in Making Jell-O Chunks. Instead of cutting the gel into chunks, cut it into fruit wedges. Arrange the wedges along the interior wall of the dessert glass. Heat some clear gel to 180°F and pour it into the center of the glass (this temperature is low enough to avoid melting the fruit wedges).

polka dot
delight

Candle gel has a look that lends itself to vivid colors and retro designs. These Polka Dot Delight candles take advantage of that fact, and the result is a fun and funky way to jazz up your décor. Dark, intense colors stand out better in colored candle gel, so avoid using very light or pastel tones for the polka dots.

what you will learn:
How to cast contrasting colors in candle gel.

special materials:
▸ candle colorants
▸ tweezers or chopsticks

MAKING THE POLKA DOT COLOR
Melt some clear gel and dye it to make the polka dot color. Pour it into a bowl and let it cool.

MAKING THE BACKGROUND COLOR
Melt some more gel and dye it to make the background color. Let it cool until it is slightly thick.

CREATING THE CANDLE
Pour a little of the background color into the container. Tear off small pieces of the polka dot color and use the tweezers or chopsticks to place them on top of the hot gel. Pour a bit more of the background color and place more chunks of polka dots with the tweezers. Continue pouring layers and adding polka dots until you near the top of the container. Add a few more polka dots on top of the background color to form small mounds.

note: To avoid having the polka dots sink to the bottom of the candle, you may have to wait several seconds in between pours to give the gel time to harden and thereby suspend the colored chunks.

A few polka dots peek out above the surface, adding texture and visual interest to the candle.

room fragrancer

Essential oils don't always work in candle gel (see page 28 for more information). But in this project they work perfectly, because the gel is used as a casting medium rather than as candle fuel. Therefore, the therapuetic qualities of the oils aren't destroyed by heat.

These room fragrancers are perfect to use in a nursery because the essential oils help lull a baby to sleep. Since the fragrancer isn't burned, you won't expose an infant's developing lungs to smoke or have a flame near an active toddler. You can also embed anything you want. Consider using bunnies, bears, ducks, or small blocks to spell a child's name.

what you will learn:
How to make a room fragrancer with candle gel.

special materials:
▶ aromatherapeutic essential oil blends (e.g. equal parts lavender and orange or equal parts orange, petitgrain, and ylang-ylang)
▶ assorted embedments

PREPARING THE GEL
To prepare the gel, double the amount of fragrance suggested in the 10 Easy Steps on page 10, as you want to increase the aroma and the higher concentration will not create a fire hazard.

CREATING THE FRAGRANCER
Do not set a wick. Glue or set the embedments in place. Pour in the melted gel and let it cool.

note: You can use an electric potpourri pot as the gel container. When the pot is plugged in, the gentle heat will help release the fragrance into the air.

Since a room fragrancer is never burned, you can embed items that are otherwise unsafe, such as these wooden and plastic toys.

embedment
enchantment

It's a fishbowl. It's a snow globe. It's a trip down memory lane!

The clarity and viscosity of candle gel make it an excellent medium in which to embed decorative items that tell a story. In this chapter, you will learn the tricks of the trade for embedding ceramic objects, glass marbles, shells, stones, and much more.

Casting little fantasy worlds in candle gel is a bit like planting a small garden or building a sandcastle — it's fun, absorbing, and very creative.

sand art

Sand is a popular additive to gel candles. It is often used to create the bottom of a seascape or to hide a wick tab from view. However, you'll use sand in this project for a different reason. You may find a container that you'd really like to use for a candle project, but the shape doesn't lend itself to sustaining a flame (see the section on containers on page 18 for more information). By filling the bottom with sand, you elevate the wick to an area in the container where it will burn easily — and you have the opportunity to create unique designs.

what you will learn:
How to use sand in gel candle projects.

special materials:
- tall or unusually shaped container
- assortment of colored sand
- bamboo skewers or other poking utensils

PREPARING THE CONTAINER
Prepare the container by filling it with layers of colored sand. Use a skewer to poke along the inside edge of the container to create a decorative design. Continue layering and poking the sand until the container is fairly full.

POURING THE CANDLE
Bury the bottom of the wick in the top layer of sand. Pour a small amount of melted gel on top of the sand to about $\frac{1}{16}$ of an inch. Let that layer cool before pouring the remainder of the gel. If you skip this step, you run the risk of having the sand rise up into the candle gel, which will cause cloudiness.

Plain and glittery sand create a nice contrast at the base of this candle.

holiday lights

Winter holidays are a popular time for festive candles and gel candle crafting can open up a whole new world of ideas for you. These candles are made with iridescent red and green glass marbles, but you can use any sort of (safe) decorations with a holiday theme that spark your imagination.

what you will learn:
How to use clear candle gel to show off embedments.

special materials:
- decorative glass container
- iridescent red and green glass marbles
- candle fragrance(s) reminiscent of winter, such as cinnamon, juniper, or pine
- liquid candle colorant(s) to match holiday theme

Iridescent glass marbles make elegant embedments for gel candles. Since they are naturally heavy, they don't need to be glued down, either.

PREPARING THE CONTAINER
Set the wick in the container. Place a few layers of marbles in the bottom of the container, keeping the wick straight. Melt some clear gel and pour it over the marbles. Let it cool.

FINISHING THE CANDLE
Melt, scent, and color the gel for the rest of the container. When the clear gel has cooled, pour in the colored gel. Use the heat technique to remove air pockets from around the marbles (see page 38).

rainbow

Candle dyes tend to bleed together. For example, if you put red wax or gel hearts in a yellow gel candle, over time the dyes will run together and the hearts will lose their distinct shape and look more like blobs. This project takes this fact of life and turns it into an advantage.

In the rainbow candle, stripes of red, blue, and yellow are clear and distinct during the first week or so of the candle's life. Over time, the colors run together, resulting in a lovely rainbow effect that would be impossible to accomplish any other way.

what you will learn:
How to manipulate candle dyes to create unique designs.

special materials:
▸ small cookie sheet
▸ razor
▸ red, yellow, and blue candle dye or premade bits of gel color nuggets
▸ scrap paper
▸ scissors

PREPARING THE GEL
Melt enough clear gel to fill a cookie sheet approximately ⅛ inch thick. Pour the clear gel onto the cookie sheet and allow it to cool completely. Use a razor to cut out three long stripes. Make sure you leave clear gel between each of the stripes. Pull the clear candle gel out of cut areas, leaving the rest of the clear gel in place. One by one, melt the red, yellow, and blue gels. Pour one color into each of the cut strips.

MAKING A TEMPLATE
Place the scrap paper inside the candle container. Use scissors to cut the paper so that it rests snug against the inside wall of the container. This paper will serve as your template for cutting the candle gel.

CREATING THE RAINBOW
When the candle gel is cool, put the paper template on top and use the razor to cut away the excess gel. Then, gently peel the candle gel away from the cookie sheet. Immediately place it against the inside wall of the container.

FINISHING THE CANDLE
Set the wick and fill the container with clear, scented gel to complete the candle. Make sure you pour the gel at a cooler temperature to avoid melting the rainbow design.

flower bouquet

This candle makes an excellent gift for Mother's Day or other special event. The shape of the brandy snifter acts like a magnifying glass, making the embedments appear larger than they really are. Molding the decorative embedments does not involve knives or heat, so this is a good project to share with children. As you work side by side, let your conversation drift into a recollection of the reasons you appreciate your lucky loved one.

what you will learn:

How to make clay embedments.

special materials:

- polymer clay (Fimo, Sculpy, or similar products, available in craft stores)
- cookie sheet lined with aluminum foil
- oven
- brandy snifter
- glass or ceramic beads

To make a bouquet of roses, roll polymer clay into angled tubes, then pinch them together.

MAKING THE EMBEDMENTS

To make the flower embedments, press the clay into flat, thin pieces. Roll them into loose, angled tubes, so that the edge of the clay forms a spiraled petal. Pinch the tubes together at the bottom. Shape more pieces into petals and attach them to the centerpiece. Pinch green clay into leaves. Make enough flowers and leaves to fill the bottom of the container. Bake them on a cookie sheet in the oven as recommended by the clay manufacturer.

MAKING THE CANDLE

Set the wick with glue and arrange the flowers at the bottom of the brandy snifter. Ploymer clay manufacturers recommend that their products be kept away from open flames. Therefore, thread a few glass or ceramic beads along the wick until they are ¼ to ½ inch above the flowers. Pour clear gel into the container, tapping the sides of the glass to help the bubbles travel upward. To remove the rest of the bubbles and make the flowers more visible, finish with the heat technique (page 38).

buried
treasure

This candle's beauty lies in the fact that it is completely free of bubbles and therefore peaceful to look at. Normally, a seascape makes for a bubbly gel candle, since the air trapped in the nooks and crannies of the sand and shells slowly rises to the surface as the gel cools. Using the heat technique (see page 38) as the essential last step in this project removes the bubbles.

what you will learn:

How to make a bubble-free seascape.

special materials:

- clean sand or dextrose-free salt
- collection of seashells, glass, and ceramic and metal embedments. note: Do not use dried starfish or other sea life. These animals eventually bloat and look unattractive.
- assortment of treasures, such as metal coins

CASTING THE SEASCAPE

Set the wick and pour the sand or salt into the container. Position the shells and buried treasure around it. Pour in the clear candle gel and immediately place the container in a preheated oven set at 220°F. Follow the heat technique as described on page 38.

Every year my friend Janie makes the long trek with her family from the deserts of Arizona to the shores of North Carolina. When she learned that I was crafting a seascape candle for this book, she sent me her beachcombed gleanings of shells and polished glass along with the suggestion that I include a coin as buried treasure. I did one better. I found a coin stamped with the year that I met Janie and tucked it near the wick. Then I attached this note: "In a world of roiling waters, I have found a peaceful place where lies a treasure as rare and precious as any gold bullion hidden in the sand — a friend."

aquarium

This little aquarium is full of life! There are fish swimming from side to side and activity all around. The key to the Aquarium candle is that various non-flammable embedments are situated at different heights throughout the container. There are many ways to accomplish this (see page 35 for more information), but this project demonstrates the simplest technique — fast-setting clear epoxy glue.

what you will learn:

How to make a lively candle montage with embedments placed at different heights.

special materials:

▸ seashells and glass, ceramic, and metal embedments. (note: Do not use dried starfish or other sea life. These animals eventually bloat and look unattractive.)

▸ fast-setting clear epoxy glue

▸ clean sand

PREPARING THE EMBEDMENTS

Prepare the seashells and embedments by washing them thoroughly and removing any bits of dirt or debris, which will cause cloudiness in the final project. Also, examine them for openings or undercuts and fill these in with glue (see page 33 for more information).

PLACING THE EMBEDMENTS

Pour sand into the bottom of the container. Glue the embedments to the interior wall of the container at various heights. You can also glue the embedments to each other. For example, glue a fish on top of a shell. When you set the shell in the sand, the fish will appear to be swimming above it or resting on it. Make sure you keep the embedments away from the wick, or the candle will not burn properly.

POURING THE CANDLE

Cast the candle as usual. Consider pouring in different colors of gel at different levels, such as light green on the bottom, light blue in the middle, and clear on top. If the final candle has more bubbles than you want, use the heat technique to remove them (see page 38).

botanical bounty

It's so pleasant to incorporate dried herbs and other botanicals into candles, but there are some real fire hazards, too. It's important to always design your candles with safety in mind.

The key to safety in this project is to set the embedments lower than the wick. You accomplish this by stringing glass or ceramic beads on the wick, until the beads are ¼ to ½ inch higher than the embedments. When the candle burns down far enough, the beads will automatically snuff out the wick before it reaches the flammable embedments.

what you will learn:
How to incorporate flammable items into a gel candle.

special materials:
- ▶ scissors
- ▶ dried chili peppers
- ▶ fast-setting clear epoxy glue
- ▶ colored peppercorns
- ▶ glass or ceramic beads

PREPARING THE EMBEDMENTS
Use scissors to trim the chili peppers to the size you would like them to be in the container. Glue the peppercorns and chili peppers to the sides and bottom of the container. If you do not glue them in place, they will become dislodged and float toward the flame as the candle burns.

CASTING THE CANDLE
String the beads along the wick until they extend ¼ to ½ inch above the top of the embedments, then set the wick. Cast the candle as usual. If there are too many bubbles and you can't see the embedments, finish the candle with the heat technique (see page 38).

It's important to glue down botanicals, or they will float upward, as shown here, creating a fire hazard. Dried materials also create lots of tiny bubbles, which disappear in time.

japanese garden

This peaceful little Japanese garden was created with ceramic embedments in the shapes of a pagoda, temple, and bridge. A layer of sand on the bottom hides the wick tab and provides a base on which to create the scene. The possibilities for thematic settings are as limitless as your imagination. Look for miniatures in stores specializing in crafts or dollhouses and you'll certainly find embedments that tell a story or illustrate a favorite hobby.

what you will learn:
How to make a thematic scene.

special materials:
- embedments with a theme
- fast-setting clear epoxy glue
- sand
- glass or ceramic beads

This small ceramic pagoda makes an interesting home for bubbles.

PREPARING THE EMBEDMENTS
If the embedments have undercuts or holes in them, seal them with clear epoxy glue so they don't create bubbles. Pour the sand into the bottom of the container and arrange the embedments on top.

FINISHING THE CANDLE
If any of the embedments are made from unsafe materials, such as wood or plastic, string beads along the wick until they are ½ inch above the top of the tallest embedment. See page 33 for more information on safe and unsafe embedments. Pour in clear gel and tap the sides of the container to help the bubbles begin their journey upward. If you want to remove some or all of the bubbles from the gel, use the heat technique described on page 38.

jewel
tones

Embedding colored candle gel in clear candle gel can be tricky. Distinct shapes tend to turn into blobs, making them hard to see. This project takes advantage of that fact by placing colored chunks of gel in a freeform, random arrangement at the bottom of the container. When you look through the clear gel from either the top or the sides, the pretty jewel tones provide an attractive, organic design.

what you will learn:
How to use candle gel embedments effectively.

special materials:
▸ candle colorants
▸ old ice cube tray
▸ wide, shallow container
▸ scissors

MAKING THE COLORED CUBES
Melt some clear gel and dye several batches various colors. Make sure that the colors are distinct yet match one another. Make one or two of the colors more opaque than the others by adding more dye. This will provide some contrast when viewing the gel embedments as a group. Pour the gel into an old ice cube tray to cool. This way, you can make small cubes to work with and you won't dirty several bowls.

ARRANGING THE GEL CUBES
If your container is very wide, you may need to set more than one wick (see page 26 for more information). When the gel cubes have cooled completely, scoop them out of the ice cube tray, cut them in half, and arrange them in the bottom of the container in a random fashion. Place the opaque cubes in strategic positions, so that they provide contrast to the more transparent cubes.

CASTING THE CANDLE
Melt some clear gel, let it cool until it becomes a syrupy consistency, and pour it on top of the colored cubes (this keeps the hot gel from melting the cubes). Tap the sides of the container to help release the bubbles.

note: Do not use the heat technique with this project, or the colors will run together.

wax
appeal

Once you realize how fast and easy gel candle crafting is, you'll be eager to go on to the next level. In the previous chapters, we explored many techniques for crafting gel candles. In this chapter, we will investigate how candle gel can be used in conjunction with other waxes as part of a more complicated candle project.

Beeswax, one-pour wax, and votive wax make lovely candles in and of themselves. However, when used in conjunction with candle gel, they can provide a range of interesting effects and serve as unique candle containers, opaque backdrops, and distinctive embedments.

sunflower
surprise

Typically, candle gel is not sturdy enough to stand on its like a regular candle. In the Sunflower Surprise project, you can overcome this limitation by encasing it in paraffin wax. While the paraffin shell obscures the beautiful transparency of the gel, the candle produces a fabulous glow when it burns. This project demonstrates the simplest way to encase candle gel in paraffin. However, with some experimentation, you may come up with your own techniques and variations.

what you will learn:
How to use the dipping technique to make a paraffin-wax container.

special materials:
▶ temporary container, such as a custard dish, waxed paper cup, or candle mold
▶ scissors
▶ paraffin votive wax
▶ double boiler (see page 51 for an inexpensive, temporary setup)
▶ fluted bowl

CASTING THE GEL CENTER
Place the wick into the temporary container or candle mold. Do not glue it to the bottom of the container, as you will later remove the gel. Pour in the melted gel. When the gel is completely cool, carefully pry it out of the container with your fingers, wick and all. Use scissors to pare the gel candle at least ¼ inch around all the sides. Try to keep the upper edge clean, but don't worry about uneven cuts or irregularities on the sides or bottom. Your goal is to make the gel candle approximately ¼ inch smaller than the container.

CASTING THE WAX PETALS
Melt the paraffin wax in the double boiler and fill approximately ⅓ of the fluted bowl with it. Immediately set the gel candle into the hot wax. This will force the paraffin up to the top of the bowl, completely encasing the gel candle. When the paraffin wax is completely cool, remove the candle from the container by turning it upside down and pulling gently on the wick.

mouth-watering
watermelon

This candle allows you to take advantage of the variations in wax and gel opacity and density. The paraffin makes a great choice for the thick, waxy rind, while the candle gel is perfect for the fleshy interior of the watermelon. Coffee beans turned on their sides look an awful lot like watermelon seeds. For this project use one-pour wax, a type of soft container wax that needs only a single pour (traditional paraffin waxes shrink when they cool and require multiple pours).

what you will learn:
How to effectively use one-pour wax in your candle designs.

special materials:
- one-pour wax
- double boiler (see page 51 for an inexpensive, temporary setup)
- green and red candle colorants
- handful of coffee beans
- fast-setting clear epoxy glue
- fragrance oil

MAKING THE RIND
Melt some one-pour wax in a double boiler and tint it a dark green shade. Pour it into a prepared container and let it cool completely.

GLUING THE SEEDS
Once the wax is cool, turn the container on its side and prop it in position so that it is stable and will not roll or move. Select the darkest and smallest coffee beans and glue a few to the inside of the container. Place the beans at various heights along the side of the container. Let the beans set completely and test them to make sure they won't move. Then rotate the container a little, prop it in place again, and glue a few more beans at various heights to the side of the container. Let the glue set completely. Keep rotating the container, gluing beans, and letting them set until you have attached beans along the interior wall of the container.

MAKING THE WATERMELON FLESH
When the coffee beans are completely set, stand the container upright. Melt some clear gel, scent it, and dye it a medium shade of red. Pour the gel into the container and let it cool completely.

stars and dreidels

Embedding colored candle gel in clear candle gel can be very pretty, but it can also be hard to see. However, if you surround gel embedments with a backdrop of opaque wax, your design will pop! The design trick to this candle is to make gel embedments that are very thick. The thicker the embedment, the more light it will reflect from both the burning flame behind it and the natural light in front of it. All this play of light makes for a candle with extra glow.

what you will learn:
How to surround gel designs with opaque one-pour wax.

special materials:
▶ aluminum foil
▶ square or rectangular container with flat sides
▶ metal cookie cutters in the shapes of stars and dreidels
▶ double boiler (see page 51 for an inexpensive, temporary setup)
▶ white one-pour wax

MAKING THE EMBEDMENTS
Create a box out of aluminum foil that has the same dimensions as one side of the container and is 1 inch high. Place a cookie cutter in the foil box in the same location it will be in the finished candle. In a double boiler, melt and scent a portion of the one-pour wax and pour it around the outside of the cookie cutter, filling in the foil box. When the wax has completely hardened, gently remove the cookie cutter. Fill in the void with colored candle gel.

CASTING THE CANDLE
While the candle gel cools, glue the wick to the bottom of the container and melt and scent the remaining one-pour wax. When the candle gel has cooled, gently remove the aluminum foil from the wax and gel embedment. Slide the entire piece into the container and press it against the interior wall with your fingers. Quickly fill the container with the remaining one-pour wax.

An assortment of cookie cutters can be used to make gel embedments in various shapes.

zen stones

This candle shows another unique way to use clear gel and opaque wax to achieve a sophisticated candle. The bottom is layered with river stones, which you can buy in most garden centers and craft stores. If you can find small stones with special messages on them, include those, too. If not, paint your own. The trick to this candle is to place the embedments at the base of the candle, use the heat technique to remove bubbles from the clear gel, and then pour wax on top.

what you will learn:
How to use the heat technique in the middle of a candle project.

special materials:
▸ river stones
▸ stones with words carved on them
▸ permanent fine-point marker (optional)
▸ one-pour wax
▸ scent and colorant of your choice (optional)

ARRANGING THE STONES
Set the wick in the container and layer the stones around it. Add a few stones with messages carved on them, or use a permanent fine-point marker to write messages on the stones. Make sure they face outward and are legible. Add a few more stones on top.

CREATING THE BOTTOM LAYER
Melt some gel and pour it into the container, covering the stones and adding another inch or so on top. Tap the sides of the container to encourage the bubbles to move upward, then let it cool. Use the heat technique to remove the air pockets and bubbles from around the stones (see page 38). Let the candle cool completely.

CREATING THE TOP LAYER
Melt the one-pour wax, scent and color it, if desired, and pour it into the container (I left the wax its natural white color for a pure, clean look).

Small black river stones and a metal message stone produce a sense of tranquility.

citrus
slices

This project reverses the process you learned in the Stars and Dreidels project (page 95), where you cast one-pour wax around the candle gel embedments to make them pop. Now you'll pour candle gel around embedments made of one-pour wax.

what you will learn:

How to make wax embedments and use the window technique to place the designs.

special materials:

▶ 2 small cookie sheets, one lined with aluminum foil

▶ white one-pour wax

▶ double boiler (see page 51 for an inexpensive setup)

▶ one small round cookie cutter

▶ four large round cookie cutters

▶ candle colorants in orange, yellow, and green

▶ vegetable peeler (optional)

▶ square or rectangular container with a "shoulder" (meaning the mouth of the container is slightly smaller than the body)

MAKING THE FRUIT SLICES

Line the cookie sheet with aluminum foil. Melt the wax in a double boiler and pour a ¼-inch layer onto the cookie sheet. When it is cool, cut out several rounds with the small cookie cutter, then use a knife to cut them into triangles. Arrange the triangles on the foil-covered cookie sheet and place a large round cookie cutter over each grouping.

Remelt the wax and pour some into paper cups. Dye the wax in each cup orange, yellow, and green. Pour the colored waxes over the wax triangles until they are completely covered. When cool, remove the fruit slices and clean them up with a knife or vegetable peeler.

USING THE WINDOW TECHNIQUE

The window technique ensures that the embedments stay exactly where you want them and protects the soft wax from the hot gel. This technique works only with square or rectangular containers where the mouth is slightly smaller than the body.

Melt the gel to 190°F. Place the container on one side and pour in a ⅛-inch-thick layer. Immediately position some of the embedments, then pour another ⅛ inch of gel on top. Let it cool, then rotate the container and repeat the process on the other sides.

FINISHING THE CANDLE

When the embedments are in place and the gel has cooled, stand the container up and cast the candle with more melted gel.

fruit
preserves

While the Citrus Slices project results in a clean, simple suggestion of jam and jelly, this project really loads up the container with wax fruits to fool the eye. You can purchase ready-made paraffin wax embedments from candlemaking suppliers, but it is just as easy to create your own. High melt-point paraffin wax is better at resisting the high temperature of hot candle gel than the low melt-point one-pour wax used in the Citrus Slices project. Even so, keep the temperature of the gel as low as possible.

what you will learn:
How to make and embed paraffin-wax designs.

special materials:
- paraffin wax
- double boiler (see page 51 for an inexpensive, temporary setup)
- candle colorants and scents to match the fruit
- candy molds with fruit shapes
- knife or vegetable peeler

MAKING THE FRUIT EMBEDMENTS
Heat the paraffin wax in a double boiler until it has melted. Color and scent it appropriately. Let the paraffin cool to approximately 130°F and then pour it into the candy molds. When the paraffin fruit has hardened, pop it out of the molds. Trim and clean the fruit with a knife or vegetable peeler.

FINISHING THE CANDLE
Set the wick and arrange the fruit in the container. Melt, scent, and color the candle gel. Allow it to cool as much as possible before pouring it into the container.

Wax embedments are available at craft stores in a wide range of shapes and colors, such as these realistic-looking fruits.

honey
pot

Due to its slight translucency, beeswax makes a really nice container for candle gel. It is also a wonderful medium to hand-mold because it is soft and pliable and has a natural aroma that warms the house as you work. Filled with honey-colored and -scented candle gel, the Honey Pot looks good enough to eat!

what you will learn:
How to hand-mold a beeswax container.

special materials:
▸ beeswax
▸ double boiler (see page 51 for an inexpensive solution)
▸ cookie sheet lined with aluminum foil
▸ small knife
▸ rubber gloves or other protective hand covering
▸ honey-colored candle colorant
▸ honey fragrance oil

MELTING THE BEESWAX
Melt the beeswax in a double boiler and pour a ¼-inch-thick layer onto the cookie sheet. When the wax has solidified but is still warm, cut a 4- or 5-inch square and peel it off. Put on rubber gloves and form the wax into a ball.

SHAPING THE POT
Place the ball on a protected countertop and flatten the bottom by pressing down. Press your thumbs into the center of the ball, creating a hole in the middle. Pinch the edges of the pot to create the rim. Continue to shape as desired until you have an empty pot.

COLORING THE BEESWAX
When the pot has cooled, remelt the remaining beeswax in the double boiler. Add the candle dye. Remove the wax from the double boiler. Hold the top of the pot with your fingers and dip the bottom into the melted wax. Repeat this until you have covered the bottom with a smooth, golden-brown coat of wax. Turn the candle upside down and repeat the process for the top of the pot.

ADDING THE HONEY
When the honey pot has cooled, fill it with honey-colored and honey-scented gel. Make sure you pour the gel at the coolest possible temperature (about 180°F) to avoid melting the beeswax. It is also important to let the container cool completely before you pour in the gel, in order to avoid a meltdown.

red, white and blue

This project shows you how to make a wax container using the pour-out technique. There are two important keys to casting these candles successfully. First, make sure that the walls of the wax containers are at least ¼- to ½-inch thick. Second, pour the gel into the wax containers at a very cool temperature to avoid cracking the wax.

what you will learn:
How to use the pour-out technique to make a wax container.

special materials:
- candle mold or toilet paper or paper towel cardboard tube
- aluminum foil
- double boiler (see page 51 for an inexpensive setup)
- pillar wax
- beeswax
- wax-lined paper cups
- old knife or vegetable peeler
- red and blue candle colorants

PREPARING THE MOLDS
A candle mold forms crisp, clean lines. If you want an organic look or don't want to buy a mold, use a cardboard tube with foil crimped around the bottom.

CREATING THE BOTTOM LAYER
In a double boiler, melt 2 parts pillar wax to 1 part beeswax. Pour some of the wax into a paper cup and dye it red or blue. Pour it into the bottom of the mold (or tube) until it is ½ inch thick. Let cool.

MAKING A WAX CONTAINER
Reheat the uncolored wax and fill the mold. Let it cool until it forms a ¼-inch skin on top. Check this by piercing the skin with a knife. Peel the skin away and pour the still liquefied wax out of the mold and into a clean paper cup to reuse for another project. You should now have a mold with a ¼-inch paraffin coating on the inside. If the wax is not thick enough, repeat this step.

SMOOTHING THE ROUGH EDGES
Smooth out the rough edges at the top of the candle with an old knife or vegetable peeler.

COMPLETING THE CANDLE
Set the wick inside the wax container and scent and color the gel with the blue or red dye. Pour in the gel, stopping ¼ inch from the top. When the candle has hardened, pop it out of the mold or tear the cardboard tube away.

summer
citronella

Citronella (Cymbopogon nardus), an essential oil distilled from citronella grass, has a mild citrus scent similar to lemon balm. The oil is a natural insect repellent but its beneficial properties can be destroyed by excessive heat. Since candle gel has such a high burning temperature, this poses a problem. One solution is to add the essential oil to one-pour wax, which burns at a relatively low temperature, and to use candle gel as an unscented, decorative element.

what you will learn:

How to incorporate scents that may not otherwise work into gel candles.

special materials:

- one-pour wax
- double boiler (see page 51 for an inexpensive, temporary setup)
- citronella essential oil
- yellow, orange, or green candle colorant
- glass planter votive holder

PREPARING THE WAX

Melt the one-pour wax in the double boiler. Scent it with citronella essential oil and add yellow, orange, or green colorant. Set the wick in the votive holder. Pour a layer of wax into the container and let it cool.

PREPARING THE GEL

Melt some candle gel and add yellow, orange, or green colorant. You may want to experiment with the shade to contrast nicely with the one-pour wax. Pour a layer of gel into the votive holder and let it cool.

ALTERNATING LAYERS

Remelt the one-pour wax and pour another layer on top of the cooled gel. Play with the thickness of the layers; they can be uniform or wildly different. Let the wax cool. Remelt the gel and pour it onto the cooled wax. Repeat these steps until you fill the container. Try making one candle in each color, varying the thickness of the stripes.

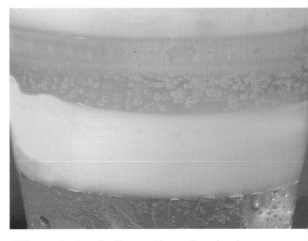

Different shades of yellow cast in candle gel and one-pour wax create these textured stripes.

from the hive

Preformed sheets of beeswax present an easy way to work with wax without melting or dyeing it. Preformed beeswax is available in a wide range of colors and, because it is so thin, you can easily cut it with scissors to form interesting shapes and designs. This is a great project for children to help with, since they can create the beeswax shapes. Be careful, though — it is very soft and pliable at even a moderate room temperature, so you'll have to pour the gel at a very low temperature and not use the heat technique on this project.

what you will learn:
How to make embedments with preformed sheets of beeswax.

special materials:
- preformed sheet of beeswax in your choice of color
- scissors
- container to match your candle theme
- yellow and red candle colorants

MAKING THE WAX EMBEDMENTS
Cut the sheet of beeswax into interesting shapes to match the theme of your candle container. Be careful to maintain the beeswax texture, which will provide an interesting contrast with the gel. Set the wick in the container and arrange the beeswax around it.

POURING THE GEL
Melt, scent, and lightly color the candle gel honey yellow with a tinge of red. Let it cool as much as possible but still be pourable. Tip the container and pour in the gel along the wall of the glass. This prevents the heavy gel from disturbing the delicate texture of the beeswax.

Slices of textured beeswax sheets and honey-colored gel look like they were just scooped out of the hive.

sea foam

Candle gel's transparency lends itself to a watery, seashore feel. This Sea Foam candle gives you another way to use candle gel and paraffin wax in a way that showcases the best qualities of each.

In addition, polished sea glass, which you can buy at art supply stores or scavenge at the beach, makes a lovely embedment that echoes the same colorful and translucent characteristics as gel.

what you will learn:
How to showcase the best qualities of candle gel and traditional wax.

special materials:
- tall container with clean lines
- several pieces of sea glass in a range of colors
- blue candle colorant
- white one-pour wax
- double boiler (see page 51 for an inexpensive, temporary setup)
- old fork (optional)

Sea glass makes a wonderful embedment because you can see through various layers of color.

CREATING THE SEA

Set the wick in the container and place several pieces of sea glass around the bottom to cover the metal tab. Layer the sea glass so you can see the various colors well. Melt some clear gel and pour it into the first third of the container. Let it cool. Melt more gel, color it lightly with a little blue dye, and pour it into the next third of the container. Let it cool.

CREATING THE FOAM

Melt some white one-pour wax in a double boiler and pour it into the last third of the container. If you wish, you can whip the top with a fork to create a more frothy appearance.

container
chic

Since candle gel is jiggly and can't normally stand alone, it is usually cast into some type of container. While this can be seen as a limitation, it is also a wonderful excuse to spend time finding and decorating a unique container to fit a certain mood.

If you do crafts with children, decorating the container gives them an opportunity to participate in your project without handling hot candle gel. This chapter includes unique ideas for decorating containers with special glass paint, polymer clay, decoupage, faux etching, glass mosaic tiles, and more.

etched
glass

Etched glass has been around for ages, but now there are special kits available in craft stores that make this art easy. You can draw designs freehand or use stencils or stamps. In most cases, you'll need to let the container dry for at least 10 days. To avoid handling the etched glass, prepare the container in advance and pour the candle gel after the etching has fully cured.

what you will learn:
How to make an etched glass container.

special materials:
▶ clear glass container

▶ glass etching kit

▶ paintbrush

▶ stencils or stamps (optional)

Kits for making faux etching designs on glass are available in craft and art supply stores.

MAKING ETCHED GLASS
Follow the manufacturer's instructions for using the etched glass kit. Apply the etching solution to the container with a paintbrush. You can draw a freehand design or use stencils or stamps. Apply the second etching solution and let the container dry for the amount of time specified on the kit's label.

MAKING THE CANDLE
Once the container has cured completely, melt, scent, color and pour the gel as usual.

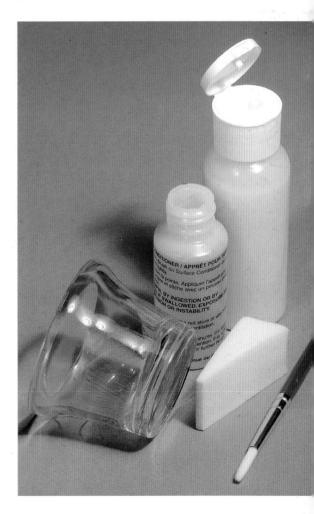

pasta
fiesta

Sometimes the best way to embed objects that shouldn't be near a flame is to put them in a separate container and place the candle container inside it. This project is wonderfully simple with regard to crafting the candle, so you can spend all your creative energies designing the surrounding display.

what you will learn:

How to use a container within a container.

special materials:

- ▶ small container for the candle that fits inside a larger container for the embedments
- ▶ fast-setting clear epoxy glue (optional)
- ▶ embedments (dried pasta, flowers, spices, beans, etc.) that you normally can't embed in candle gel

Certain items, such as this dried pasta, are better off placed in a separate container and not embedded in candle gel.

MAKING THE CANDLE

Cast the gel candle in the small container. Set the candle in the middle of the larger container. You may want to glue the containers together with clear epoxy glue so they don't slide around.

ARRANGING THE EMBEDMENTS

Arrange the embedments in the gap between the two containers.

optional: Pour clear candle gel into the gap between the containers to hold the embedments in place. Skip this step if you are using dried botanicals, fresh flowers, and other delicate items, as hot candle gel can char and destroy them.

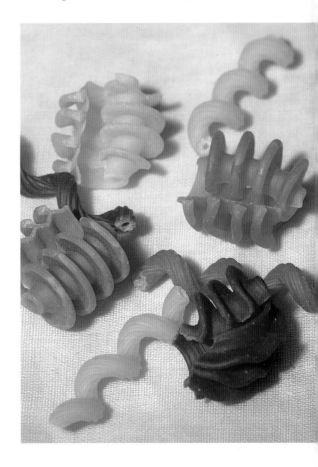

uncanny candles

This project allows you to recycle your used cans and your candle gel at the same time. Recycling is good for both the planet and the candle crafter.

Sometimes you may tint a batch of candle gel too heavily or contaminate it with sand or other debris from project mistakes. The best use for such gel is to hide it from view by casting it into a metal container. No one will know what the gel really looks like, and the cans add a nice retro look to your décor.

what you will learn:
How to use a metal container.

special materials:
▶ collection of interesting metal containers

COLLECT OLD CANS

Recycle old cans by washing them thoroughly. Make sure they have no rough edges left along the rim.

CASTING THE CANDLE

Collect old candle gel from other projects that you can't use in a glass container. Melt the gel and pour it into the prepared metal containers.

Empty, clean cans can be recycled as gel candle containers for a unique look.

painted glass

If you have some artistic talent, hand painting a container can add a lot of value to your candle project. Hand painting increases the price tag of your work by making the container reusable for other things, such as holding flowers or knickknacks, long after the candle is gone. It also allows you to customize the candle for an event or a person. For example, you could paint small glass containers with the names of guests at a birthday party. The candles can then be used as place cards that guests take home after the party is over.

If your painterly talents are limited, consider using sponge-painting techniques, stencils, stamps, or a few well-placed brush strokes.

MAKING A TEMPLATE

Place the paper inside the container, spreading it out so that it rests flat against the interior walls. You may have to use scissors to cut the paper to the right size. Remove the paper and draw your design on it with a pencil. Put the paper back inside the container and tape it firmly in place.

PAINTING THE CONTAINERS

Use glass paint and a paintbrush or special pens and other devices for drawing on glass to paint the design. Or use sponge-painting techniques, stencils, stamps, or brush strokes to make a design. Cast the candle as usual.

what you will learn:
How to hand paint glass containers.

special materials:
► white paper
► container with smooth sides
► scissors
► pencil
► tape
► glass paint and paint brushes or pens and other devices for drawing on glass (available from craft stores)
► stencils, sponges, and stamps (optional)

altar ego

This project shows you how to use paper decoupage to transform a simple container into a reflection of your spirituality. You can use just about any paper item in your paper decoupage design, such as torn swatches of handmade paper or cutouts from magazines or old greeting cards. If you have access to a color photocopier or a scanner and color printer, make copies of leaves, flowers, and other items from nature.

what you will learn:
How to make paper decoupage containers.

special materials:
- container
- paper and pencil
- bits of paper cut or torn from stationery, magazines, and greeting cards
- paper cup
- white glue
- paint brush (optional)

SELECTING THE CONTAINER

If you plan to completely cover the container with decoupage, you can use a ceramic or metal container and fill it with leftover scraps of gel, as in the Uncanny Candles project on page 119. If you use a glass container, consider covering only a portion of the container so that light and colored gel can shine through your design.

MAKING A TEMPLATE

Roll the container over the paper, using the pencil to outline its shape. Arrange the decorative items and trace them on the paper in a design that appeals to you.

APPLYING DECOUPAGE

In the paper cup, mix equal amounts of white glue and water. Dip the paper scraps into this mixture with your fingers and then affix them to the container, using the paper template as a guide. Or paint some glue-water onto the container with a brush, affix the scraps of paper, and apply a final coat of the mixture. Let the container dry overnight, then cast the candle as usual.

clay art

This project uses a special type of translucent polymer clay to decorate the outside of a container with a motif. You simply roll out the clay with a rolling pin, cut out shapes with scissors, press them against the glass, and then bake them in the oven until hard. Since the container isn't completely covered in clay, you can hone your design to integrate the colors of the clay with the colors of the candle gel. This is a simple and fun project to do with small children.

what you will learn:
How to use polymer clay to decorate a container.

special materials:
▸ paper and pencil

▸ tracing paper (optional)

▸ Fimo's translucent polymer clay designed for application to glass

▸ rolling pin or round glass

▸ oven

Special clay that adheres to glass is a perfect medium for decorating gel candle containers.

MAKING A TEMPLATE
Choose a basic color scheme and motif design (you may want to consult some books for ideas). Roll the container over the paper, using the pencil to outline its shape. Transfer the design to the paper using tracing paper or sketch it freehand.

MAKING THE CLAY DESIGNS
Roll out the clay to about $\frac{1}{16}$-inch thick with a rolling pin or a round glass. Use the paper template as a guide to cut the polymer clay shapes to size with a craft knife. Press them lightly onto the paper to form the design. Gently peel the shapes off the paper and press them onto the exterior of the container. Set the oven to the temperature recommended on the product's label and bake the clay until it is hard, following the directions of the manufacturer. Cast the candle as usual.

glass
mosaic

If you are working with a flat-sided square or rectangular container, you can jazz it up by gluing decorations to the exterior in a mosaic design. Utilizing items that both block and reflect light adds a new level of complexity to the candle's flame.

To make a mosaic, purchase bits of glass from a craft store or glass retailer. You can make the container even more unique by interspersing the glass with other decorative items, such as marbles, shells, costume jewelry, and broken bric-a-brac, to create a hodge-podge tour de force. As you design the mosaic, remember that you can play with color by using different hues of candle gel inside the container.

MAKING A TEMPLATE

Roll the container over the paper, using the pencil to outline its shape. Arrange the bits of glass and seashells on the paper in a design that appeals to you.

CREATING A MOSAIC DESIGN

Lay the container on its side and glue the decorative items to the container, following your paper template as a guide. When the glue has dried, rotate the container onto another side and affix more mosaic glass to the container. Let the glue dry completely, then continue decorating one side at a time until the container is covered. You can also try with leaving areas uncovered, or covering just the rim or the base of the container. When the glue has dried completely, cast the candle as usual.

what you will learn:
How to make glass mosaic containers.

special materials:
► flat-sided container
► paper and pencil
► glass mosaic tiles, sea glass, marbles, and other bits of glass
► seashells (optional)
► mosaic tile adhesive or fast-setting clear epoxy glue

containerless
floating candles

Candle gel is normally too jiggly to stand on its own without a container. But if you cast small floating candles out of extra-firm candle gel that you make yourself, you should have no problems. The only trick to making floating candles is that they must be relatively small (otherwise they will sink). Also, the candle will both float and burn better if the bottom is wider than the top.

what you will learn:
How to make your own candle gel.

special materials:
- 1 lb. white mineral oil with a flash point of 375°F and a viscosity of 200
- 1.4 oz. thermoplastic resin powder CP9000
- unique molds, such as small gelatin molds
- sharp utensil, such as an ice pick, bamboo skewer, or heavy-duty dressmaker's pin
- large bowl for floating candles
- glass fish or flowers (optional)

MAKING STAND-ALONE CANDLE GEL
Mix the mineral oil and resin and let the mixture sit for one hour. Stir the mixture until all the lumps are gone. Heat the mixture to 220°F on the stovetop. As it heats, it will turn clear. (See page 131 for more recipes and information on making your own candle gel.)

CASTING THE CANDLES
Pour the mixture into the molds. Do not set the wick, as the candle needs to be turned upside down in order to be wider at the base than at the top. Remove the cooled candles from the molds by gently peeling them away. Use a sharp utensil to pierce the middle of the candle and then thread a wick through the hole.

FINISHING THE CANDLES
You may wish to dip the candles in some more melted gel in order to seal the wick in place. To do this, hold the candle by the wick and dip it once into the hot gel. Trim the wick and arrange the candles in a bowl of water with some fresh flowers.

note: To jazz up your floating candle display, add food coloring to the water. By placing glass fish or other inflammables in the bowl, you can transform a simple bowl of water into a pond full of life as well as light.

crafting as a business

As with may hobbies, gel candle crafting can be as simple or as complex as you wish to make it. Often, the most beautiful creations are the easiest to produce. What makes them appealing is an exquisite fragrance, an unusually lovely color, or a creative concept. If you decide to turn gel candle crafting into a business, here are some key points to keep in mind:

▶ Use high-quality, appealing fragrances, colors, and containers.

▶ Keep your raw materials cost low. The containers and embedments are the most expensive items and the most likely ones to cut into your profit margin.

▶ Keep your designs simple enough to mass produce. The cost of labor can quickly make a candle too expensive to manufacture.

▶ Join an Internet chat group that focuses on gel candle crafting. You may meet people with all kinds of tips and advice.

▶ Always include a warning label with every candle you sell.

▶ Don't price your candles too low.

▶ Have fun.

making your
own candle gel

Some crafters may want to make their own gel so they can control the density and viscosity.

ingredients

▶ White mineral oil with a flash point of 375°F and a viscosity of 200
▶ Thermoplastic resin powder CP9000

squeezable candle gel
(after making the gel, pour it into a plastic bag, snip off one corner of the bag and squeeze it into the container around the wick. This gel requires no heating.)
1 lb. mineral oil and 0.1 oz. resin

low-density candle gel
1 lb. mineral oil and 0.9 oz. resin

medium-density candle gel
1 lb. mineral oil and 1.1 oz. resin

high-density candle gel
1 lb. mineral oil and 1.25 oz. resin

stand-alone candle gel
(doesn't require a candle container)
1 lb. mineral oil and 1.4 oz. resin

This custom-made candle gel is formulated to be dense enough to stand alone and does not require a container.

instructions

1. Mix the proper proportions of mineral oil and resin. Let the mixture sit for one hour.

2. Stir the mixture well until all the lumps are gone.

3. Heat the mixture to 220°F on the stovetop. As it heats it will turn clear.

4. Pour the mixture into a jar and let it cool. Seal the jar with a tight-fitting lid.

metric
conversion charts

Unless you have finely calibrated measuring equipment, conversions between U.S. and metric measurements will be somewhat inexact. It's important to convert the measurements for all of the ingredients in a recipe to maintain the same proportions as the original.

approximate metric equivalents by volume

u.s.	metric
1 teaspoon	5 milliliters
1 tablespoon	15 milliliters
¼ cup	60 milliliters
½ cup	120 milliliters
1 cup	230 milliliters
1¼ cups	300 milliliters
1½ cups	360 milliliters
2 cups	460 milliliters
2½ cups	600 milliliters
3 cups	700 milliliters
4 cups (1 quart)	0.95 liter
1.06 quarts	1 liter
4 quarts (1 gallon)	3.8 liters

approximate metric equivalents by weight

u.s.	metric
¼ ounce	7 grams
½ ounce	14 grams
1 ounce	28 grams
1¼ ounces	35 grams
1½ ounces	40 grams
2½ ounces	70 grams
4 ounces	112 grams
5 ounces	140 grams
8 ounces	228 grams
10 ounces	280 grams
15 ounces	425 grams
16 ounces (1 pound)	454 grams

approximate U.S. equivalents by weight

metric	u.s.
1 gram	0.035 ounce
50 grams	1.75 ounces
100 grams	3.5 ounces
250 grams	8.75 ounces
500 grams	1.1 pounds
1 kilogram	2.2 pounds

general formulas for metric conversion

Ounces to grams	multiply ounces by 28.35
Grams to ounces	multiply grams by 0.035
Pounds to grams	multiply pounds by 453.5
Pounds to kilograms	multiply pounds by 0.45
Cups to liters	multiply cups by 0.24
Fahrenheit to Celsius	subtract 32 from Fahrenheit temperature, multiply by 5, then divide by 9
Celsius to Fahrenheit	multiply Celsius temperature by 9, divide by 5, then add 32

product specifications for penreco candle gel

VERSAGEL C PROPERTIES

	low polymer	medium polymer	high polymer
Approximate Flash Point	440°F (227°C)	440°F (227°C)	440°F (227°C)
Approximate Pounds per Gallon @ 77°F (25°C)	7.0	7.0	7.0
Recommended amount of Glitter or Specialty Pigment	Not recommended	No more than 0.3%	No more than 0.3%
Recommended Fragrance Load	0–4%	3–6%	3–6%

Source: Penreco Company

mail-order resources

Helpful Web Sites

Alphabetcrafts.com
This resource site provides links to various craft sites on the Internet.

Alphabetwax.com
This educational site offers tips, ideas, projects, and links on gel candle crafting.

Gel Candle Supplies

Bath and Candle Supplies.com
215 North Main Street
Clarion, IA 50525
(866) 272-3957
www.bathandcandlesupplies.com

BioMax of Ohio
99 Corbin Mill Drive
Dublin, OH 43017
(800) 752-5052
www.biomax1.com

Bittercreek Candles
Route 4, Box 184
Ashland, WI 54806
(877) 635-8929
www.candlemaking.net

Bobby's Craft Boutique
120 Hillside Avenue
Williston Park, NY 11596
(516) 877-2499
www.craftcave.com/candle/can-home.htm

Cajun Candles
P.O. Box 784
Kaplan, LA 70548
(800) 667-6424
www.cajuncandles.com

Candle Factory Co.
5449 N. State Road 7
Tamarac, FL 33319
(954) 714-1000
www.candlefactoryco.com

Candle Factory Products
1130 Ship Avenue
Beachwood, NJ 08722
www.candlefactoryproducts.com
service @candlefactory
products.com

Candlemaker
1210 Highway 246 South
Greenwood, SC 29649
(864) 223-3645
www.angelfire.com/sc/candle-maker

The Candlemakers Store
6077 Far Hills Avenue #167
Centerville, OH 45459
(937) 428-9323
www.thecandlemakersstore.com

Candles and Supplies.com
301 S. 3rd Street, Rt. 309
Coopersburg, PA 18036
(800) 819-6118
www.candlesandsupplies.com

Candlewic Company
8244 Easton Road
Ottsville, PA 18942
(610) 847-2076
www.candlewic.com

Georgies Ceramic & Clay Co.
756 NE Lombard
Portland, OR 97211
www.georgies.com
info@georgies.com

Glorybee
120 N. Seneca Road
Eugene, OR 97402
(800) 456-7923
www.glorybee.com

Jane's Small Gifts
P.O. Box 32126
Mesa, AZ 85275-2126
(480) 833-8830
www.janessmallgifts.com

Juniper Tree
2520 San Pablo Avenue
Berkeley, CA 94702
(510) 647-3697

Kewl Candle Factory, LLC
1829 S. Kingshighway
St. Louis, MO 63110
(314) 477-5258
www.gelcandlesupply.com

Majestic Mountain Sage
881 West 700 North, Suite 107
Logan, UT 84321
(435) 755-0863
www.thesage.com

Missy's Candles
366 US Route 35
Ray, OH 45672
(740) 884-4516
www.candlemaking.com

Penreco
910 Louisiana, Suite 400
P.O. Box 4274
Houston, TX 77210
713-236-6950
www.penreco.com

Polygon Wax
200 West 2nd Street
P.O. Box 348
S. Boston, MA 02127
(617) 268-4455
www.polygonwax.com

Pourette
P.O. Box 70469
Seattle, WA 98107
(800) 888-9425
www.pourette.com

Silky Tyme
P.O. Box 3068
Santa Fe Springs, CA 90670
(562) 301-5120
www.silkytyme.com

Starrville Soap Works
6180 Highway 271
Tyler, TX 75708
(903) 533-0199
www.starrvillesoapworks.com

Swan's Candle Supplies
8933 Gravelly Lake Drive SW
Tacoma, WA 98499
(253) 584-4666
www.swanscandles.com

TKB Trading
356 24th Street
Oakland, CA 94612
(510) 451-9011
www.wholesalecolors.com

Yaley Enterprises
7664 Avianca Drive
Redding, CA 96002
(530) 365-5252
www.yaley.com

Fragrance and Essential Oils

Angel Sky Products
4644 County 18
Hazen, ND 58545
(701) 748-5710
www.angelskyproducts.com

Bramble Berry, Inc.
301 W. Holly, Suite M6
Bellingham WA 98225
(360) 734-8278
www.brambleberry.com

Herbal Accents
560 N. Coast Highway 101, Suite 4A
Encinitas, CA 92024
www.herbalaccents.com

Mint Meadow

Country Oils
N 8573 Highway H
Camp Douglas, WI 54618
(608) 427-3561
www.members.tripod.com/~mint-meadow/index.html

Rainbow Meadow
P.O. Box 457
Napoleon MI 49261
(517) 764-9795
www.rainbowmeadow.com

Self Essentials
8142 A Junipero Street
Sacramento, CA 95828
(916) 388-9575
www.selfessentials.com

Senna's Bath and Garden
919 8th Avenue South
Nampa, ID 83651
(208) 463-4717
www.sennas.com

SoapBerry Lane
317 W. Palmyra Drive
Virginia Beach, VA 23462
(757) 490-8852
www.soapberrylane.com

Sweet Cakes Soapmaking Supplies
18 North Road
Kinnelon, NJ 07405
(973) 838-5200
www.sweetcakes.com

Glassware for Gel Candles

Couronne Company, Inc.
501 W. Powell Lane #404
Austin, TX 78753
(800) 573-4367
www.glassnow.com

Heavenly Scents
38734 Reinninger Road
Denham Springs, LA 70706
(225) 791-9266
www.glassware4gellin.com

Embedments for Gel Candles

Amazing Gel Candle Embeds
17465 Cross Street
Lake Elsinore, CA 92530
www.gelembeds.com

Anette's Cookies-N-Candles
51430-3 Tiguas Drive
Ft. Hood, TX 76544
(254) 539-1209
http://anettescookiesncandles.com

Wicks

Wick n' Clip
1513 Lincoln Avenue
Holbrook, NY 11741
(631) 471-9425
www.wicknclip.com

Wicks Unlimited
900 Sylvan Avenue
Bayport, NY 11705
(631) 472-2010
www.wicksunlimited.com

index

other storey titles
you will enjoy

The Candlemaker's Companion, by Betty Oppenheimer. The clear, illustrated instructions in this book show readers how to create rolled, poured, molded, and dipped candles; add scent, color, and decorations; and use special techniques, such as overdipping, painting, layering, and sculpting. 208 pages. Paperback. ISBN 1-58017-366-7.

The Handmade Candle, by Alison Jenkins. This beautifully photographed book has clear and simple instructions for making designer candles at home at a fraction of the retail cost. Includes more than 20 projects using a variety of molds, decorative embellishments, special effects, and dazzling patterns. 80 pages. Hardcover. ISBN 1-58017-353-5.

Making Natural Liquid Soaps, by Catherine Failor. With this easy hot-process soapmaking technique and a few simple, pure ingredients, readers can create liquid soaps that are better for their skin and better for the environment. Includes recipes for moisturizing hand soaps, revitalizing shampoos, invigorating shower gels, soothing bubble baths, and gentle baby and pet shampoos. 144 pages. Paperback. ISBN 1-58017-243-1.

Making Transparent Soap, by Catherine Failor. Beautiful photographs and clear text offer readers a thorough exploration of this soapmaking technique. Includes recipes and tips for crafters to make stunning transparent soaps in their own kitchens. 144 pages. Paperback. ISBN 1-58017-244-X.

Melt & Mold Soap Crafting, by C. Kaila Westerman. Soapmaking has never been this easy! The revolutionary melt-and-mold method is taking the craft world by storm. Beginning with a meltable glycerin base, readers can create fabulous specialty soaps in minutes — it's as easy as melt, pour, mold, and decorate! 144 pages. Paperback. ISBN 1-58017-293-8.

These titles and other Storey books are available at your bookstore, farm store, or garden center, directly from Storey Books, 210 MASS MoCA Way, North Adams, Massachusetts, 01247 or by calling 1-800-441-5700. Or visit our Web site at www.storey.com